AUSTIN SEVEN

ROGER BUGG

AMBERLEY

Acknowledgements

This book has been compiled under unusual circumstances, which have placed so many restrictions on movement and gatherings. By courtesy of the Austin Seven Clubs Association I have been allowed to make free use of the A7CA magazines, and other material held in the Archive at Lubenham. Chris Garner and Hugh Barnes have been most helpful in my researches. Fellow members of the Pre-War Austin Seven Club have provided archive photos from their collections and permission to photograph their cars, where possible. In particular I should like to thank Neville Barr, Brian Shaw, John Skeavington, David Astle, Ron Bailey, Dave Dye, Geoff Roe, Graham Beckett, David Martin, David Mann, John Debens, Phil Baildon, Jonathan Cooper, Andrew Neale, Paddy Malone, John Gray, Tony Pearson, Bill Tull, Chris Gould, Mike Hodgson, Nick Turley, Mike Costigan, Derek Chatto and Roger Mallinson.

Every effort has been made to trace copyright holders and ensure that no copyright has been wittingly infringed.

First published 2023

Amberley Publishing
The Hill, Stroud,
Gloucestershire, GL5 4EP

www.amberley-books.com

ISBN: 978 1 3981 0985 8 (print)
ISBN: 978 1 3981 0986 5 (ebook)

British Library Cataloguing in Publication Data.
A catalogue record for this book is available from the British Library.

Typeset in 10pt on 13pt Celeste.
Typesetting by SJmagic DESIGN SERVICES, India.
Printed in the UK.

Contents

Introduction 5

1 **Setting the Scene** 6
Austin and Longbridge 7
Forerunners and Competitors to the Seven 7
Society in the 1920s and 1930s 8

2 **Genesis of the Austin Seven** 12
Designing the Car – Stanley Edge 12
Launch of the Seven 14
Public Reception of the Seven 15
Promoting the Seven 15

3 **Features of the Models** 17
The End of Production 30

4 **Development of the Seven – Racing** 32
Rivalry with MG 39

5 **Sevens Under Licence** 43
Specialist Bodybuilders 43
Sevens Abroad 44
Military Sevens 47
The Seven Engine Adapted for Land, Sea and Air 49

6 **Road Tests** 52

7 **The War Years and Post-war Austerity** 64
The 750 Motor Club and Specials 64
The MOT and the End of the Road – the Phoenix Arises 67
Specialist Suppliers for Special Builders 69
Technical Advice Sources 72
Spares Suppliers 72

8 Motoring in a Seven through the Decades 75

9 The Austin Seven Motors On 83
Finding an Austin Seven 90

Appendices 94
Useful Contact Points 94
Other Sources of Information – Booklist 94

Introduction

'The war to end all wars' had only ended just over three years before the Austin Seven first made its appearance. The war had changed the world forever. The motor car, hitherto the preserve of the rich, was now something that all could aspire to but few yet could hope to own. Not only were big, luxury cars unaffordable for most to buy, but the RAC formula introduced in 1910 of a £1 tax on horsepower rating made them very expensive to run. Motorcycles and combinations existed but were hardly suitable for the lady of the house to be seen on. What was needed was a car that would provide all the features of a bigger car but still be affordable by the 'man in the street'. No manufacturer had so far produced such a car. This tricky problem was solved by Herbert Austin and Stanley Edge. Together they created a car that not only met the needs of a new motoring public but has remained a favourite ever since – the Austin Seven.

Chummy crossing Nettleham Ford, Lincolnshire, 2011.

1

Setting the Scene

The antecedents of car design may be traced back to cycle manufacturers and carriage makers. The cycle industry was relatively new and innovative. It had developed hub brakes, variable gears, differential axles (in tricycles) and use of ball bearings. When John Boyd Dunlop reinvented the pneumatic tyre in 1887 it was first used for cycles not cars. Cycles were usually limited to one or possibly two riders and had to be as light as possible to reduce the amount of effort required by the rider or riders. Steel tubes in triangulated designs were used for lightness and strength. The influence of the cycle industry is clearly seen in early motor cars.

Herbert and his brother in a first Austin Tri-car, 1895.

Many motor manufacturers began their careers in the cycle industry. BSA, Citroen, Clement, Lea-Francis, Morris, Riley, Rover, Singer, Star, Sunbeam, Swift and Triumph all made cycles originally. However, as with all new things, it was the rich who first made use of them. They demanded something befitting their status in society. It was obvious that traditional carriage design would be their preference because greater loads could be carried in greater comfort. The horseless carriage provided space for passengers, luggage and somewhere for the chauffeur to sit. The chassis had to be substantial enough to carry the body weight, which in turn required larger and more powerful engines. Until the 1920s it was the rich who dictated what a motor car should be – big, luxurious and exclusive. The age of 'small is beautiful' had not yet arrived.

Austin and Longbridge

The Longbridge site south of Birmingham had been taken over from a print company by the Austin Motor Company in 1905. Initially it had been only 4 acres, employing around a thousand workers. During the war years Longbridge expanded as it switched to munitions production. By the end of the war it covered 40 acres and the workforce was around 20,000. When government contracts for munitions ceased the plant had to be returned to its former purpose of making cars. This was not a straightforward process. Not only was the existing plant unsuitable for peacetime purposes, but the layout of the site was not ideal for mass production. Despite these problems, in July 1919 Sir Herbert followed Ford's one-model policy when he introduced the Twenty. Demand was high for any new car in the immediate post-war years and the Twenty was solid, well-made and reliable, but after the post-war boom had subsided there was a general slump in demand. Sir Herbert was obliged to introduce the smaller Twelve version of the Twenty. This was also a reliable and comfortable car. In taxi form it remained a familiar sight well into the 1950s. Although cheaper to tax and run than a Twenty, the Twelve was still well beyond the means of the average man. In 1920, an unskilled worker might receive around £1 a week and a skilled worker around £2 a week.

Forerunners and Competitors to the Seven

Attempts to find a way to build smaller cars had been made throughout the Edwardian period. These had produced the cycle car. Although cheaper to buy and run, cycle cars were generally crudely constructed, with flimsy bodywork. However, the Peugeot Bebe of 1912 and its successor in 1920, the Quadrilette, included features later to be found in the Austin Seven. The chassis was triangulated, with a transverse front spring. The Quadrilette had a four-cylinder in-line water-cooled engine of 667cc. Unlike the Seven, the body initially only offered two staggered seats. Sir Herbert was probably aware of these cars as he was a French speaker and often travelled to France.

One car Sir Herbert was familiar with was the Rover 8, which had been introduced in 1920. It also came from a cycle car background with a two-seater body and a twin-cylinder air-cooled engine. It sold well for few years, but by 1925 the public no longer wanted noisy, air-cooled engines. The 8.7hp GN was also a cycle car, with an air-cooled twin-cylinder engine. The long-lived 7hp Jowett had a two-cylinder water-cooled flat-twin engine. The 8hp Gwynne offered an innovative overhead-valve engine, and Wolseley offered an 8.3hp two-cylinder model.

All of these were competitors to the Austin Seven, as it sought to gain a niche in the market. Price reductions for the Seven were made possible once assembly line production got underway and gave it the edge over its rivals. New challenges occurred in 1927 when Singer introduced the 8hp Junior with an overhead-valve engine. In 1928, Triumph produced an 8hp car with a three-bearing engine, and Morris introduced the 8hp Minor with an overhead-valve engine. In 1932, Ford produced the Model Y with a 933cc side-valve engine, their first model specifically for the European market. In terms of actual market competition, the Morris Minor offered a more advanced engine, especially when modified for use in MGs, and the Ford Model Y offered price savings. By 1935 it was offered at £100 for the basic model. However, the popularity of the Austin was not seriously diminished by its rivals.

Society in the 1920s and 1930s

The 1920s and 1930s saw a huge increase in the development of suburbia, with its confusion of styles from mock-Elizabethan to Art Deco. Despite the economic slump of the late 1920s and most of the 1930s, those who were not made unemployed enjoyed a golden age in which home and car ownership became a distinct possibility. With land cheap, available and saddled with few planning regulations, most new homes could be bought for less than £750 at a time when the average wage stood at about £165 a year.

Chummy in Suburbia.

In retrospect, the 1920s marked the end of the golden age of motoring. In 1923, there were only 385,525 cars on the roads in Great Britain. By 1930 the number topped one million. Within another eight years another million cars were added. Today the figure is around thirty-two million. Demand for car ownership was growing rapidly. It opened up far wider opportunities for travel, not just for business purposes but for pleasure. It was still an adventure to find one's way to far off places and discover the joys of the country and seaside. A side effect of increased motor travel and higher speeds was the number of road casualties. This led to the hitherto uncoordinated mass of legislation designed for the age of the horse and cart being codified in 1931 into the Highway Code. Driving tests did not arrive until 1935. By the 1930s the road system had been classified and numbered into A for trunk and other main roads, B for minor roads and U for unclassified to cover everything else. The programme of road surfacing had extended to all but country lanes. There were even some dual carriageways. Manually controlled traffic lights were first used in London in 1926 and an automatic trial system was used in Wolverhampton in 1927.

Motoring in the 1920s, Buckler's Hard, Hants.

Between Edge Hill and Sunrising Hill, 1920s.

Motoring in Britain a century ago differed in so many ways from today that it is hard now to imagine an age where horse-drawn traffic was commonplace; there were no motorways, yellow lines, speed cameras, seat belts or driving tests. What motorised transport there was consisted of motorcycles, lorries, buses and cars, all restricted to 20mph, even though most cars were capable of 35–40mph. Garages supplied fuel from hand-cranked pumps. There were few filling stations. Manufacturers supplied tool kits as standard with new cars. Cleaning the plugs, changing a wheel or de-coking the engine were a normal part of car ownership in those days.

Left: Motoring in the 1930s. A family of six in a 1929 Saloon.

Below: Motoring in the 1940s. Boat Tail in Bures High Street, Essex.

Above: A 7CA roadside picnic in the late 1930s.

Right: A Ruby being filled up, 1930s.

2

Genesis of the Austin Seven

Sir Herbert not only had to contend with the problems of designing an economic, soundly constructed and reliable small car, but overcoming hostility to the idea from the directors of the Austin Company. They saw no future in such a radical departure from Austin's current larger models. However, sales for the Twenty were falling and the Twelve, introduced in 1922, had yet to establish itself. The company was £2.25 million in debt. Things were so bad that a receiver was appointed in 1921 to look at the Austin finances. It was not an ideal time for Austin to ask his fellow directors for backing to build an entirely new model, unlike any previous design.

However, Sir Herbert was not so easily dissuaded. His Works Director Charles Englebach and Financial Director Ernest Payton worked with him to try and resolve the financial crisis quickly. At the same time the problems with the Longbridge site were progressively addressed. The various factory buildings on opposite sides of the railway were connected by a road bridge. Machinery was then grouped so that entire sub-assemblies could be completed on one site, with quality control centralised from start to finish. Thus, when the sub-assemblies were united there were no delays due to incompatibility of parts. This reorganisation was carried out between 1924 and 1927 at a cost of £600,000, while maintaining production throughout. Sir Herbert continued to develop ideas for an economy car. Initially his thinking favoured a 6hp cycle car, along the lines of the successful 8hp Rover. The directors would not agree to finance this, however. Sir Herbert had to decide whether to finance the scheme himself or possibly take manufacture elsewhere. At this point there began an association with a young man who would enable Sir Herbert to realise his idea for 'a large car in miniature'. Without this meeting it is likely the car that emerged would have been very different and far less successful. If credit for the concept of a small but fully equipped car must go to Sir Herbert, the realisation of his ideas must go to Stanley Edge.

Designing the Car – Sir Herbert Austin and Stanley Edge

Stanley had joined Austin as a junior draughtsman at the age of fourteen upon leaving school in 1917. He was a keen motorcyclist but was also fascinated by British and

Continental engine and car design. At the time of their first discussions Sir Herbert would have been nearing sixty years of age, with many years of experience in designing and building motor vehicles. Stanley, aged just eighteen, had no previous experience of design or production, but possessed a wide knowledge of current developments in the motoring world. Austin must have become aware of his knowledge, coupled with enthusiasm for his chosen career. The two would meet before other staff arrived in the drawing office, where Stanley worked. This gave them the opportunity to discuss ideas for a practical small car design. The meetings began in mid-1920 and continued for about a year. Sir Herbert had already sketched his ideas for a small car. The earliest shows an X-frame chassis with a four-door body. A later sketch has the familiar A-frame chassis, with the front axle attached at the apex and located by radius arms. Both sketches show a four-cylinder in-line engine. The air-cooled horizontal twin engine originally favoured by Sir Herbert had gone. Stanley acknowledged many years later that his own thinking had been influenced by the 748cc four-cylinder in-line engine used in the Belgian motorcycle FN Type 700, first introduced in 1914. The gearbox was attached to the rear of the engine, and, in keeping with FN practice, shaft drive was used rather than a chain. Crank and gearbox cases were aluminium. All these features were to be incorporated in the Austin Seven.

Stanley's task was to turn Sit Herbert's sketches into detailed drawings. In September 1921, he left the Drawing Office in Longbridge to work for Sir Herbert at his home at Lickey Grange. During the week Stanley slept in the coach house. This

Stanley Edge and his Connaught motorcycle, 1921.

arrangement lasted until April 1922. As Sir Herbert's personal assistant rather than a Longbridge employee, the work could be done without the knowledge of the directors. Sir Herbert's sketches were reasonably accurate and detailed, but Stanley could see where they derived from the 8hp Rover, which he knew Sir Herbert had examined closely at Longbridge. With his knowledge of current engine design, Stanley was able to convince Sir Herbert that a water-cooled four-cylinder engine was preferable to the noisy and rough-running air-cooled two-stroke engine of the Rover 8, and would cost no more to build.

By the beginning of 1922 the configuration of chassis, transmission and final drive had been agreed. It was left to Stanley to calculate the most suitable designs for the engine, gearbox and clutch. Apart from engines specially modified for racing, the side-valve engine he designed was to remain the standard unit throughout the production run. Its original modest performance was essentially designed for use in a car for the family man. However, once production began the potential for modifying the engine for sporting and racing purposes was quickly realised. Transmission, steering and brakes were outside Stanley's experience, and here Sir Herbert could advise how to scale down from larger cars.

The demand for Stanley to produce finished drawings was enormous. Work continued day and evening, and even at weekends. Each part of the car was meticulously drawn. The engine and gearbox were followed by the front and rear axles, chassis frame and body. The completed drawings were taken to Longbridge in April 1922. Sir Herbert had previously had an area boarded up in which the first three prototype cars were to be constructed. Stanley moved back to Longbridge to work on the prototypes. These were to be completed by the beginning of June. By then the directors had agreed to fund the project, and Sir Herbert managed to take a royalty of 2 guineas on every Seven sold.

Launch of the Seven

The world first became aware of the new car on 21 July 1922 at a press reception at Claridge's Hotel in London. Sir Herbert described the new car as, 'A decent car for a man who, at present, can only afford a motor-cycle and combination.' At the annual dinner of the Birmingham Motorcycle Club, he rather tactlessly prophesied the Seven would 'kill' the large family combination motorcycle. The wider public got the chance to see the Seven on the Rootes Ltd stand at the Motor Show held from 3 to 11 November 1922 at Olympia.

At Longbridge many staff, accustomed to the much bigger Twelves and Twentys, regarded the new car with dismay. When Eric Gordon England visited Longbridge to discuss possibilities for racing, Sales Manager Holbrook told him: 'The whole thing's a bloody nonsense – they'll never sell any of them.' According to Stanley Edge, a similar view was expressed by William Rootes of Rootes Ltd – at that time Austin's main agents. He told Sir Herbert, 'My dear Sir, the public will just not stand for this,' to which Sir Herbert replied, 'My dear Sir, I am educating the public.' There was clearly quite a lot of educating to be done. Hitherto small cars had been seen as cheap and nasty, and mass production was viewed with scepticism. However, far from ruining the company, the Austin Seven remained in production for seventeen years and was instrumental in bringing motoring to the masses.

Public Reception of the Seven

Sir Herbert modestly, and perhaps fairly, did not claim to have inspired the trend towards smaller things, but simply that the Austin Seven had come along exactly when the public demand was for a 'small compact, highly-manoeuvrable vehicle which provides all the modern motorist requires in performance and accommodation, and now possesses a reputation for reliability unexcelled by even the most reliable large-car in the past.' Naturally, the public took some time to become accustomed to the Seven. It is far easier to scoff at something different than to appreciate its virtues. The earliest Sevens were referred to as 'bathtubs on wheels'. However, even the jokes served to promote the car, and, with price reductions, sales rose. By the end of 1926 production exceeded that of the Twelve.

At the mid-point in the production run of the Austin Seven – 1932 – Sir Herbert gave a speech to the Society of Motor Manufacturers and Traders. His talk was entitled 'The Small Car meets the Modern Need'. Sir Herbert referred to the need for manufacturers to provide products suited to the tastes of the public and awareness of the economic climate. His aim was to provide the best possible product within the means of the intended market. He noted that the tendency was to build smaller not only because advancing technology made it possible but general utility made it preferable to older, larger designs. In 1932, nearly half of all new registrations were for 10hp cars or under. The 8hp tax bracket alone made up 25 per cent of all new registrations. Clearly these were the cars of choice, and Sir Herbert made the point that 'ignoring cost, the small car would still lead in popularity on account of its size, and all the allure it possesses as a consequence'. Production of the Seven continued to rise, reaching its peak in 1935, with approximately 23,500 cars made in that year.

Promoting the Seven

To gain acceptance it was essential to prove that the Seven was no mere novelty but capable of undertaking sustained journeys on any roads, and still showing fuel economy even when fully laden. *The Advocate*, the Austin house magazine, promoted the car through endorsements from satisfied customers. A promotional booklet 'The Motor for the Million' appeared in 1923. This Seven was pictured as a second car for people who could already afford a car, to be used by the lady of the house or for 'getting down to the golf club' or for a servant to run errands. Whatever the early advertising suggested, the real market lay among first-time buyers. The Austin Seven was quintessentially designed for the man with a young family, anxious to get behind the wheel of a small but fully equipped motor car. Despite their initial scepticism, Rootes Ltd, as Austin's main distributor, were soon advertising the Seven as offering 'big car comfort at little expense'. Hire purchase was possible, with payments from £4 a month. They didn't say how many months, but with a buying price of £165 it would probably have been over three years.

Rootes advertisement, 1929.

3

Features of the Models

Whether Sir Herbert was aware of or remotely interested in current ideas of form following function and putting the most in the least possible space, it is certain that the Seven achieved those aims. However, the earliest Sevens still retained some characteristics of cycle car design. No fan, electric starter, windscreen wiper or shock absorbers were fitted initially. The triangulated chassis was made from the best materials – light but of great strength. The front axle was also triangulated by use of radius arms. The 696cc four in-line cylinder engine was water-cooled. The three-speed gearbox connected to a jointed prop shaft driving a conventional crown wheel and pinion back axle. Unusually for the 1920s, 6in-diameter brakes were fitted to all four wheels, the fronts and rears operating independently. Electric lighting was standard from the start. Despite its tiny size, the body could carry two adults and two children in reasonable comfort, with a proper hood and side screens.

Improvements to the original design began almost immediately. As the Seven fell in the 8hp tax bracket, it was logical to increase the engine size to the maximum possible without going above 8hp. This was done by increasing the bore to 56mm and the stroke to 76mm. This produced an engine of 747cc, which, even allowing for re-bores, was just under the 750cc limit for Class H competition purposes. Problems with over oiling were cured by changing the oil rings. The original Scintilla magneto was replaced by the BLIC model, which proved better for running at low speeds. From the outset the engine had provision for mounting a fan and these were fitted from October 1923. An electric starter became standard from December 1923. The very short, straight gear stick was lengthened to make it more accessible for drivers to reach. The transmission was modified so that the prop shaft was driven via a fabric coupling and thence via a universal joint to the torque tube and back axle. Crown wheel and pinion design had to be modified after problems with gear stripping. The back axle ratio was standardised with a 9/44 pinion and crown wheel. Hartford shock absorbers could be obtained as extras from mid-1923, and Austin produced their own self-adjusting shock absorbers on all cars from mid-1925. The chassis was strengthened to cope with the demands placed upon it in August 1926, and extra struts were fitted on the rear cross member. Extensions began to be fitted to the frame channels from August 1927 to support the rear of the body. It was also realised that 6in-diameter brakes were insufficient even by the modest road speeds of the 1920s, and the diameters were increased in September 1926 to 7ins. One feature that was not addressed until almost the end of production was the very short clutch travel. Until drivers became accustomed to this the car could jerk forward alarmingly. The entertainer George Clarke made a successful variety act out of it.

In September 1928, coil ignition superseded the original magneto design. The crankcase was redesigned. At the same time the original $1\frac{1}{8}$in crank was strengthened to $1\frac{5}{16}$ins. In June 1936, a three-bearing crank replaced the two-bearing type hitherto used. Further alterations had to be made when the petrol tank shifted to the rear of the car in September 1932. In place of the gravity-fed system a manual petrol pump, driven off the camshaft, was fitted to the crankcase. The starter motor moved from inside the front seat area to the offside of the engine bay.

The original design of the chassis and engine were so well conceived that they required relatively few changes over the nearly two decades of production. The original 6ft 3in chassis wheelbase was extended in October 1931 to 6ft 9ins to allow larger bodywork to be carried with more space in the rear. This also required the back axle to be widened. In July 1934 the standard 19in wheels were replaced by 17in wheels, which lowered the height of the chassis. Raised extensions carried the rear-mounted petrol tank. Coupled brakes, so that all four operated together, were fitted from July 1930. It was not until August 1936 that semi-Girling brakes were introduced. The brakes remained cable-operated until June 1938 when a stronger rear axle was fitted with Girling brakes operated by rods. The gear lever also went through changes. The original quadrant-mounted gear stick was replaced in October 1929 by a longer rod-type lever without the quadrant. The three-speed crash gearbox, which often required some skill to effect a smooth gear change, was replaced in September 1932 by a four-speed box, and synchromesh was added on the second, third and fourth gears in August 1933. For the first couple of years wheels designed for 26×3.00in beaded edge tyres were used, but these were replaced in 1924 by well-based rims for 3.50×19in wired edge tyres. From September 1926 closed centre hubs were used, but in June 1931 these were replaced by open centre hubs with Staybrite caps.

The only bodywork offered initially was the open Chummy style, intended for two adults and two children. Allowing for the fact that the average height and weight were less in the 1920s, the space was just about sufficient to travel in modest comfort. By comparison with other cars on the market, the body was tiny. However, it was strongly made of wood-framed aluminium, with steel wings and running boards. The hood and side screens offered far more comfort than any motorcycle combination or cycle car. At a total length of 9ft 2 inches and a width of only 3 feet 10 inches the Seven was only half the size of a Twenty. It was also less than half the price. Initially it weighed approximately 8½cwt but could carry 30–32 stone. However, with the 747cc engine it soon proved itself capable of producing speeds up to 50mph and 10½bhp.

In February 1926, the body design was superseded by a slightly larger one, with a more complex hood frame. The scuttle and screen were redesigned and a four-piece bonnet replaced the earlier, more awkward to handle, three-piece version. Headlights remained on the windscreen pillars. In 1926, a saloon version of the Chummy was offered. In August 1928, both Chummy and Saloon bodies were restyled to coincide with the introduction of coil ignition. The scuttle gained ventilators and the headlights moved forward to the front

George Clarke – 'His First Car'.

AC Chummy, 1925.

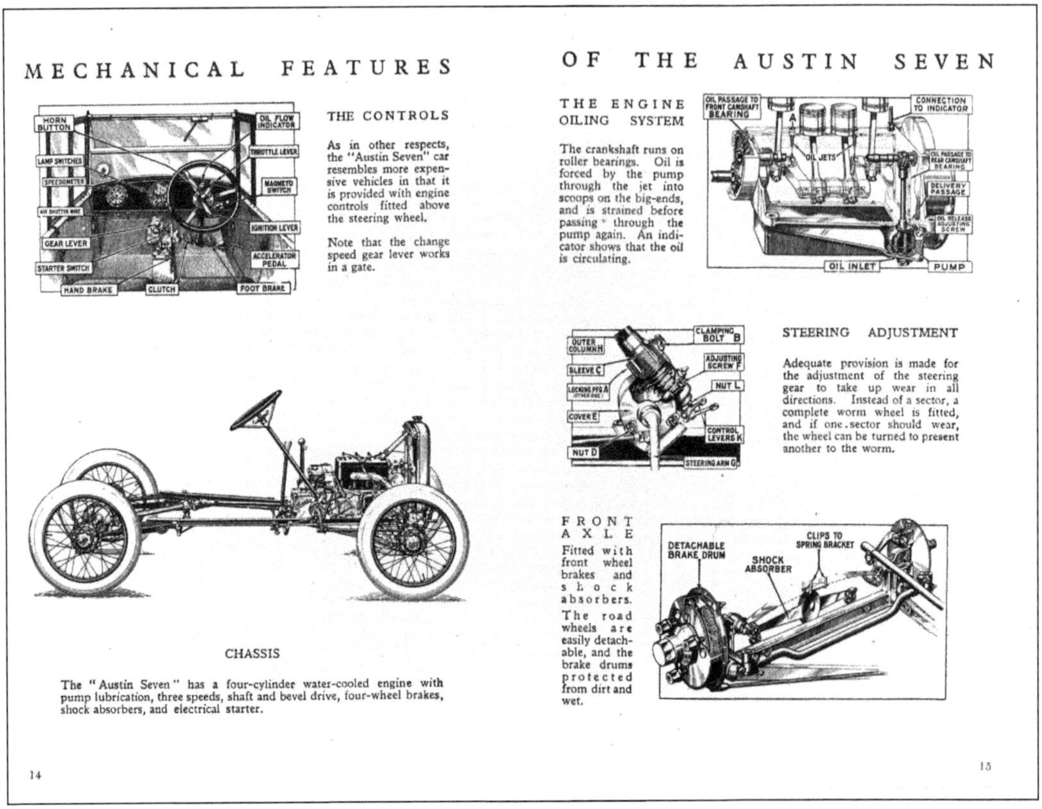

MECHANICAL FEATURES OF THE AUSTIN SEVEN

THE CONTROLS

As in other respects, the "Austin Seven" car resembles more expensive vehicles in that it is provided with engine controls fitted above the steering wheel.

Note that the change speed gear lever works in a gate.

THE ENGINE OILING SYSTEM

The crankshaft runs on roller bearings. Oil is forced by the pump through the jet into scoops on the big-ends, and is strained before passing through the pump again. An indicator shows that the oil is circulating.

STEERING ADJUSTMENT

Adequate provision is made for the adjustment of the steering gear to take up wear in all directions. Instead of a sector, a complete worm wheel is fitted, and if one sector should wear, the wheel can be turned to present another to the worm.

CHASSIS

The "Austin Seven" has a four-cylinder water-cooled engine with pump lubrication, three speeds, shaft and bevel drive, four-wheel brakes, shock absorbers, and electrical starter.

FRONT AXLE

Fitted with front wheel brakes and shock absorbers. The road wheels are easily detachable, and the brake drums protected from dirt and wet.

14

15

Above: 1926 chassis.

Left: 1927 AD Chummy.

R-type 1927 Saloon.

wings. A slightly taller nickel, later chrome, radiator replaced the earlier black shell. The deeply dished steering wheel was replaced by a flatter version.

From May 1930 the first of the steel-bodied saloons was produced, having more stylish wings, a longer bonnet and taller chrome radiator. In June 1930, a Tourer version was introduced. Both cars used the standard 6ft 3in chassis. However, by June 1930 the age of

1929 chassis.

Above: 1929 AE Chummy.

Below: 1929 RK Saloon.

Right: 1929 Fabric Saloon.

Below: 1929 Coupe.

1929 PB Boat Tail two-seater.

Gordon England Cup model.

aluminium (or fabric) and ash body construction was nearly over. The demand for open bodies, favoured in the 1920s, was also in decline. Bodywork became increasingly more stylish, in keeping with changing public tastes. The flowing lines of the steel-bodied cars reflected the popular Art Deco style.

In October 1931, a longer body was introduced on a 6ft 9in chassis. This offered more space for passengers in the back seat. The 'Box Saloon' styling remained until

Above: 1930 RL Saloon – no ventilators or louvres.

Right: 1931 PC Boat Tail.

the introduction of the Ruby Saloon in July 1934. This was the first of Austin's Jewel range. The familiar Austin radiator cowl disappeared and for the first time the radiator was enclosed within the body styling. Smaller 17in-diameter wheels were used, and the chassis lowered in consequence. Front and rear bumpers were fitted to the De Luxe models. A Pytchley sliding roof (previously an optional extra) was standard. In July 1936, a slightly revised version of the Ruby was introduced, with a three-bearing crankshaft. The other members of the Jewel range were the Pearl Cabriolet, the Opal two-seater Tourer and the four-seater Open Road Tourer.

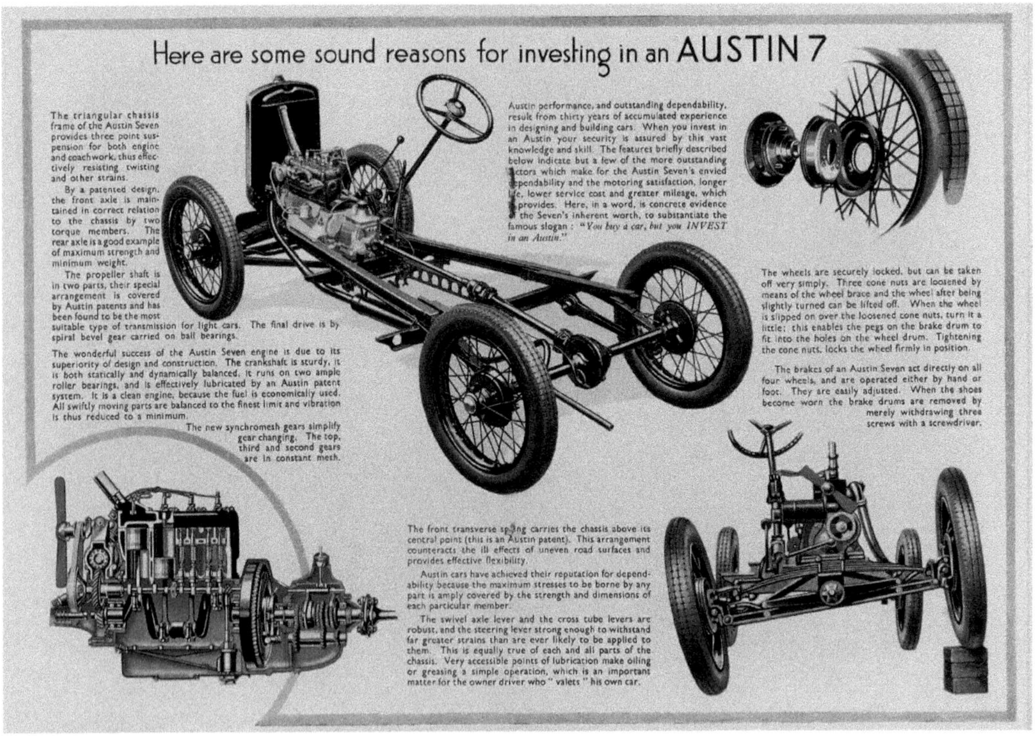

Above: Long wheelbase chassis and engine.

Left: 1932 RN Saloon.

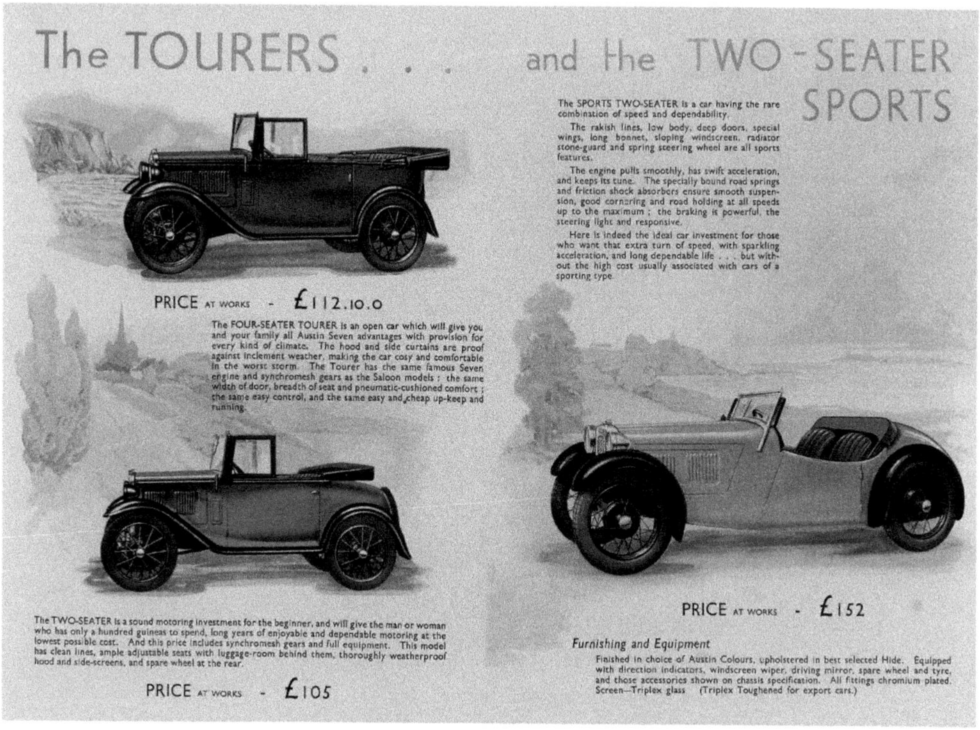

Above: 1934 Tourer, PD Tourer and Sports two-seater 65.

Below: 1933 RP Saloon De Luxe.

1937 low-frame chassis.

1934 ARQ Ruby Saloon.

1936 ARR Ruby.

1936 Pearl Cabriolet.

1936 Opal.

The adaptation of the Austin Seven for commercial uses began almost as production got underway. In October 1923 a 2½cwt delivery van was added to the Austin Seven range, with bodywork made by Thomas Startin Ltd of Birmingham. From 1930 vans were wholly made at Longbridge. From 1928 a small number of vans were also made by Gordon England. In general, the various mechanical improvements were put into the vans slightly later than the cars, possibly a case of using up stock parts. However, the van retained the chromed radiator cowl until July 1937 when it was finally enclosed as on the other models. By the end of production in 1939 the carrying capacity had increased to 5cwt. Many other adaptations for commercial use were offered, including taxis, milk floats and salesmen's cars.

The End of Production

The Austin Seven remained in production for seventeen years, from 1922 until 1939, almost as long as the Model T Ford. Unlike Ford's one-model policy, the Seven was only part of the Austin model range. It succeeded because it was able to find a new market among those who had not previously been able to afford a car. It became progressively more affordable due to the rationalisation and re-equipping of the Works. From an initial price of £225, by 1923 it had dropped to £165, and by 1928 the Chummy was priced at £125 and the Saloon at £135. These prices then remained fairly constant throughout the 1930s.

Production increased yearly from less than 2,000 in 1923 to nearly 24,000 in 1930. From then on figures began to plateau, apart from 1935 when production reached nearly 28,000. However, by then it was clear that the Seven had reached the end of its life as a production model. Sales began to decline and in 1937 the Big Seven was introduced, which bore little relation to its forebear apart from the name. By 1939 the last Sevens left Longbridge. The Big Seven was itself replaced by another new model in that year – the Austin Eight. No more private cars were produced for the duration of the war, but the Austin Eight continued for military use. When engine production ceased at Longbridge, Reliant purchased the manufacturing rights, jigs and tools to use in their three-wheeler vans.

Above: 1937 5cwt van.

Below: 1939 Reliant three-wheeler van.

4

Development of the Seven – Racing

From the start the potential of the Austin Seven chassis and engine for racing purposes was recognised. The first appearance of an Austin Seven in a sporting event occurred on 29 July 1922, when one of the prototype cars driven by Lou Kings ascended Shelsley Walsh in 89.8 seconds, coming third on formula. The performance was not lost on Arthur Waite, Sir Herbert's son-in-law, who was head of the Experimental Department at Longbridge. A racing driver himself, he was keen to develop the Seven, and was in the right place to access components and cars for test designs. Eric Gordon England, also a racing driver and car designer, visited Longbridge in 1922 specifically to persuade Sir Herbert to allow him to develop the Seven. Sir Herbert himself was no stranger to racing. Over a decade earlier in 1908 a team of four Austin racers had been sent to compete in the French Grand Prix. These were developed from the 60hp touring model. Only two of the cars survived the race, in 18th and 19th positions.

Working separately, Waite produced his car for the opening meeting at Brooklands on Easter Monday, 2 April 1923. Waite drove his car, a fabric-covered ash-framed two-seater with a back axle ratio of 4.5 to 1, from Birmingham to Brooklands in Surrey on the morning of the race. He won the race at an average speed of 59.03mph. The outcome of Gordon England's visit to Longbridge achieved two things. Firstly, he persuaded Sir Herbert that racing was the only way to convince the public of the capabilities of the Seven. Secondly, he managed to obtain a running chassis to modify in time for the Brooklands Whitsun Meeting on 21 May 1923. The car Gordon England built had a streamlined single-seater body, improved breathing and fuel flow, Hartford shock absorbers and a back axle ratio of 4.5 to 1. In the race he averaged 73.5mph for the hour and 64.79mph for the 100 miles. Sir Herbert was convinced, and Gordon England was asked to race officially for Austin. The Works Racer, built by Waite, could not equal this or other performances achieved by Gordon England. From then on Sevens and racing were never far apart. Waite and Gordon England continued to race both at home and abroad. Gordon England developed his ideas from his works in Putney, London, while Arthur Waite had a works team at Longbridge to design, build and race Sevens. Success on the track helped to sell cars, provided the racers remained essentially Sevens at heart.

Gordon England had a new car ready to race at Brooklands in October 1923. This was a two-seater with a fabric-covered body. Its success led in June 1924 to it being marketed as the 'Brooklands' Super Sports. Sir Herbert was so impressed by the performances of Gordon England's car on the tracks that he not only advertised but allowed them to be sold through Austin agents. Not to be outdone, in January 1924 the first Austin-built sports model was marketed, with similar features to the fabric Works Racers produced in 1923. A modified Seven floor pan carried a two-seater aluminium body, with flared wings and a graceful tail.

In August 1925, Gordon England introduced his Cup Model, which was designed for both competition and road use. The two-seater body had ash frames covered in thin ply. When the Wembley exhibition closed at the end of October 1925 Gordon England moved

Above: 1923 Fabric Racers.

Right: 1924 Sports Model.

his production from Putney to the now empty Palace of Industry. The Cup Model could be supplied with a standard Seven engine or a modified Brooklands. It was to remain in production until 1929.

Building on experience gained in racing, in November 1927 Austin produced the Super Sports Model. The engine had a Cozette supercharger with a stiffer counter-balanced crankshaft and high-lift cam. It could produce 27bhp at 4,500rpm – nearly three times that of a standard engine. In 1929, four cars were entered for the Ulster Tourist Trophy Race held on 17 August. The drivers were Fraser Nash, Coldicutt, Barnes and Holbrook, under the management of Gordon England. Against far larger rivals with top racing drivers, the Austins succeeded in completing the thirty laps of the 14-mile course. Fraser Nash was third at an average speed of 59.60mph, Holbrook fourth at 59.49mph, Barnes sixteenth at 56.65mph and Coldicutt nineteenth at 55.77mph.

In 1930, the Ulster TT took place on 23 August, with three Austins entered, driven by Poppe, Waite and Frazer Nash as the works team. A fourth Austin was entered separately driven by Crabtree. A crash and engine failures meant that only Poppe finished, in fifth place. By the time of the BRDC 500 miles event at Brooklands in October 1930 improvements to crankcase and block had been made. On 4 October 1930, SCH Davies and

1928 Gordon England Cup.

Above: 1928 Super Sports, driven by S. V. Holbrook.

Right: 1929 Ulster in road-going condition.

the Goodacre drove a 747cc supercharged Seven to win at an average speed of 83.41mph. On 15 October 1930 the car was again used by Davies and the Earl of March at Brooklands, and broke thirteen Class H records.

Both Waite and Gordon England had shown what could be done to improve the Seven's performance. However, Waite returned to his native Australia in January 1927, and Gordon England had ceased to manufacture cars by 1930 when the demand for his plywood construction bodies was superseded by all-steel bodies.

Capitalising on successes in the Ulster Tourist Trophy, in February 1930 Sir Herbert marketed a Sports two-seater Type EA, which later became known popularly as the Ulster. This was available un-supercharged and supercharged. The two-seater body was made from aluminium over an ash frame. To add strength, no doors were fitted. The chassis

1929 Works Team TT car.

was lowered by bowing the front axle and flattening the rear springs. Although only a few hundred cars in total were produced, many replicas have been built over the years. It was the epitome of what a small vintage sports car should be.

Sir Herbert followed the Ulster in 1933 with the aluminium-bodied EA 65 two-seater. Unlike the Ulster, this had doors and a boot lid, and was fundamentally a road car. The following year the aluminium body panels were replaced by steel, and the cars were called Nippies. The same year the short-lived 75 Speedy appeared. Success in racing was still considered necessary to help promote standard models. Three Speedys were entered in the MCC Land's End Trial as 'Special Austin Sevens'. The body styling was altered to reflect the successful Singer cars of the time. They were known unofficially as 'Grasshoppers'. A further four cars were built to compete in the 1935 Le Mans 24 Hour Race. These retained side-valve engines but benefited from three-bearing crankshafts and improved cylinder heads, designed by Murray Jamieson. However, the works team was not very successful, and it was a privately entered Speedy driven by John Carr and Jack Barbour that put in the best performance. They completed 141 laps of the circuit, finishing ahead of Dodson and Richardson with 138 laps.

Four more cars were built for Le Mans in 1936, but due to industrial unrest in France it was not until 1937 that three of the cars appeared there. The works team was Bert Hadley and Charles Dodson, Charles Goodacre and Denis Buckley, and Kay Petre and G. Mangan. All three cars had to retire before the end of the race due to engine failure. However, the cars were modified again for Reliability Trials and were successful in the twelve-hour event at Donington in 1937, taking second, third and fifth places. Grasshoppers were never sold commercially, and, with the production life of the Seven nearing its end, the cost of running a works team was no longer viable.

1934 EA Sports 65.

1935 EB Nippy.

Above: 1935 EK 75 Speedy.

Below: 1937 Grasshopper in the Colmore Trial, Hadley and Simpson.

Rivalry with MG

By the time that the Morris Minor appeared in May 1928, William Morris had had ample time to realise there was considerable demand for a small car and to see how he could improve on the six-year-old Seven design. The Minor had an 847cc overhead-valve engine (replaced by a side-valve version in 1930) and a slightly bigger body, offering more comfort than a Seven but for a similar price.

Cecil Kimber, manager of Morris Garages in Oxford, had been modifying standard Bullnose and Cowley Morris models since 1922. The advent of the Morris Minor offered an opportunity to develop a small MG based on the Minor. The M-type MG, introduced in 1928 with its fabric-covered two-seater body, was to prove not only a rival to the Austin works team cars but also a successful seller in the marketplace. Kimber's purpose was fundamentally different from Sir Herbert's in that success in racing meant more sales of MG sports cars. Sir Herbert wanted success in racing to promote the reliability and versatility of the standard Seven.

1929 MG M type.

By the end of 1930 some of the Class H records held by Austin were lost to an un-supercharged MG Midget driven by George Eyston. Worse was to follow. On 10 February 1931 at Montlhery, George Eyston was the first person to exceed 100mph over a measured distance in a 750cc car. Austin's best effort had been at Daytona Beach in April 1930 when Donald Campbell had managed 94mph in a single-seater. The works team faced further disappointment in the JCC Double-Twelve held at Brooklands on 8 and 9 May 1931. The supercharged Austins were heavily handicapped against the un-supercharged MGs, which took the first five places. In the Irish Grand Prix, held on 5 and 6 June 1931, the MGs again swept the field. However, Kimber's decision to supercharge his MGs, and thereby compete on equal terms with the supercharged Austins, was not rewarded. In the Light Car Club's Ninety-lap Relay Race held at Brooklands in June 1937, the works team won at an average speed 81.77mph – and won the MG trophy.

The Austin team had been planning a new single-seater in 1931, but Sir Herbert demanded that it should retain a side-valve but supercharged engine, mounted in the traditional A-frame chassis with transverse front and quarter-elliptic rear springs. On 8 August 1931 Leon Cushman in *Yellow Canary* at last exceeded 100mph to take the British Flying Kilometre and Mile 750cc records. There were eventually three cars built of this type, which became known as 'Dutch Clogs' or 'Rubber Ducks' from their toy-like appearance. At Montlhery in September 1931 Gwenda Stewart broke four Class H records, including 109.13mph for 5 kilometres. At the Brooklands Easter Meeting in 1932 Len Driscoll broke the lap record at 103.11mph.

1934 side-valve single-seater.

1937 Nuffield Trophy. Petre, Goodacre and Hadley.

Murray Jamieson, twin-cam single-seater.

In the search for ever higher speeds MG moved ahead again with a Flying Mile recorded at 118.83mph in early 1932 at Pendine Sands in South Wales. The Austin 'Rubber Duck' engine could not be developed further to beat this figure. However, at this point Murray Jamieson, who had joined Austin in 1932, produced a new engine design from first principles capable of withstanding the enormous stresses placed on it at high speeds. The new side-valve engine was built into a streamlined shell on the existing 'Duck' chassis design. In October 1933 this car achieved 119.30mph at Montlhery. MG again broke this record, only for Pat Driscoll of the works team to raise the speed yet again to 122.74mph on Southport Sands, breaking the World 1km record. However, the limits had been reached for development of the side-valve engine. Sir Herbert was insistent that cars developed for racing should still be recognisable as Austin Sevens, with A-frame chassis, axles and springs. Jamieson's new design had the four cylinders arrange in vee formation, and overhead valves. The new Twin-Cam Racer appeared in late 1935. Three cars were built and competed with varying degrees of success until August 1939 when Bert Hadley won the Imperial Trophy at Crystal Palace. Racing success had doubtless helped promote the Austin Seven, and the rivalry with MG was genuine and serious. However, with the end of production of the Seven, a works team was no longer justified. The age of 'the right crowd and no crowding', used to promote Brooklands, was over. For the less well off there were hill climbs, where enthusiasts could show off their cars and skills. However, there was as yet no club specifically catering for people keen to emulate the achievements of the works teams.

5

Sevens Under Licence

Specialist Bodybuilders

The 1920s were the heyday of specialist bodybuilders. The Seven chassis could be bought from Longbridge for £115 in 1925, reduced to £112 in 1926, and £94 10*s* in 1931. Any firm could use one as a basis to carry a body of its own design. Using aluminium or fabric with ash framing, many small firms had the facilities to build a wide variety of body types. The most successful were Gordon England, who offered the Cup Model from 1925, followed by the Stadium Sports and a Fabric Saloon. His bodies used a box-girder plywood floor bolted to the chassis at only three points. They were ideally suited to the Austin Seven chassis and engine, being light, strong and immune from the twisting of the chassis. The more notable of the other specialist providers were Swallow Sidecars, later to become Jaguar, who from May 1927 produced their very distinctive and smart saloons and two-seaters. Mulliner of Birmingham also produced fabric-covered coupes and saloons from 1927, and a Sports version in 1928.

Gordon England Fabric Saloon.

Left: Swallow two-seater.

Below: 1930 Mulliner two-seater.

Sevens Abroad

In February 1927, the Dixi Werke AG of Eisenach, Germany, approached Austin for permission to manufacture the Seven under licence but adapted to suit German requirements. Austin co-operated in this to enable mirror-image chassis and engines to be produced. By the beginning of 1928 production began of the Dixi DA1 Phaeton, with coil ignition and forward-mounted headlights. Early in 1928 Dixi was taken over by BMW.

In 1928, in France, SA Automobiles L. Rosengart acquired the right to build Austin Sevens under licence at their factory in Neuilly. A cabriolet version appeared in June 1928 known as the Rosengart 5cv 'Le Bebe'. Gallic influences included three seats (the rear one mounted sideways) and wheel discs.

1927 Dixi 3 15 Saloon.

1928 Rosengart Sports LR2.

In February 1929, the American Austin Car Company acquired rights to manufacture the Austin Seven under licence. It was hoped that following the economic crash of 1929 the public taste would be for smaller and more economical cars than hitherto seen in America. Despite great enthusiasm for what was seen as a novelty, sales of the American Austin never reached projected figures. Saloons, coupes and roadsters were available, closely modelled technically on the Austin Seven, but with smoother body styling to conform to American tastes. Bumpers were fitted. The company hoped to produce 60,000 cars a year, but production never reached 10,000, and continued to fall as the Depression worsened. It was not enough to keep the factory in Butler, Pennsylvania, fully occupied. By 1932 it was forced to close and American Austin was bankrupt. Eventually it was able to reopen under new management as American Bantam in 1936. Production continued until 1941 when the factory was turned over to war production.

The connection between the Dat Automobile Manufacturing Company of Osaka, Japan, was somewhat obscure. Datsun advertised their new Roadster as 'our first car manufactured in 1933 under licence'. Austin Sevens were imported to Japan from 1928, and Datsun may have been influenced by the chassis and 750cc engine design. Bodywork of the cars was similar, being scaled-down versions of the Box Saloon and later the Ruby. A Datsun was examined at Longbridge and Sir Herbert advised Datsun that the Austin Seven was protected by patents. It is probable that an agreement was reached whereby Datsun could use specific Austin patents in return for a royalty.

1929 American Austin Roadster.

1937 Datsun Saloon.

Military Sevens

The Armistice of 1918 and the uneasy interwar years made it inevitable that the Seven would be adapted for military purposes. The Mulliner Military Seven was introduced in March 1929 to replace motorcycles used for scouting purposes. The chassis and engine were slightly modified to suit British Army specification. The bodies were steel and had only a single door, on the nearside. The rear of the body was squared-off to hold military equipment. Longbridge produced its own Military Tourer from 1934, based on the standard APD model.

In Germany in April 1929 BMW produced its own scout car, the DA2 3/15PS Military Personnel Car. Anything larger was prohibited under the Versailles Treaty. It was basically the production BMW two-seater adapted to carry military equipment. This included dummy tank sides, the real thing not being allowed.

The forerunner of the Willys/Ford Jeep used in the Second World War was an experimental vehicle built by the American Bantam Car Company. Although not adopted, the military did take note, and devised a specification for a four-wheel-drive general-purpose vehicle. Bantam succeeded in producing prototypes at short notice in 1940. When America entered the war in December 1941, Willys and Ford also built the Jeep to the military specification.

Above: Mulliner Austin Military Seven.

Left: 1929 BMW Dixi Military Seven.

The Seven Engine Adapted for Land, Sea and Air

George Brough used the Seven engine and gearbox in his Brough Superior BS4 motorcycle in late 1931. Engine and gearbox were conventionally mounted to drive a twin back wheel. At £188 it was far more expensive than a standard Austin Seven, and only remained in production for a few years.

With interest in boating increasing, Messrs Maintenance Ltd of Hammersmith, who were Austin tuning specialists, introduced the Austin Seagull Motor Launch in early 1930, in which they fitted a modified Austin Seven engine into a hull built for them by the Moorcar Boat Co. of Faversham. This generated sufficient interest that around 1935 Austin produced their own Thetis and Triton engines, which were marine versions of the production Austin Seven and Ten engines respectively. A similarly converted Austin Seven engine was also offered in the late 1930s by Elephant Motors Ltd of Newington Causeway in South London. Surviving engines all date from 1924, which suggests a job lot of old stock was purchased.

The Austin Seven engine played its part in aviation. A magneto engine, built from two scrap engines, was used as a starter for the Gloster E28 jet aircraft, designed by Sir Frank Whittle. In the early 1920s Austin produced the Henri Mignet-designed 'Flying Flea' light aircraft, believed to have used the Seven engine. At least eight are known to have been built. Charles Cooper bought his plane as a kit of parts in the 1930s, and flew it successfully, until they were banned due to fatalities. A spare engine was used to build into his son John's Special for his twelfth birthday in 1935.

Above: 1931 Brough Superior.

Right: Elephant Motors Marine Engine.

Cooper 'Flying Flea', 1936.

The Seven engine was also adapted to power railway inspection trolleys. D. Wickham of Ware, Hertfordshire, modified Chummies in the mid-1920s by fitting flanged wheels and locking the steering. However, Chummy bodies and chassis were not intended for rail use and suffered badly. Purpose-built locos with Austin Seven engines were used successfully on a number of industrial narrow-gauge lines or in miniature steam-outline locos in amusement parks.

Modified Sevens were used for all kinds of manufacturing, agricultural, horticultural and forestry work. Light tractors could be constructed by modifying bodywork, axles, wheels and gearboxes.

Austin Seven-powered loco at Sylva Springs, Hants.

1940s tractor.

6

Road Tests

From the start, the motoring press was not slow to give its opinions based on practical experience. Road tests provided independent assessments of new models, a helpful guide for intending purchasers. Today they indicate what was considered worth commenting on at the time of publication. One of the first appeared in *The Light Car and Cyclecar* for 15 July 1922. The car used was clearly one of the prototypes, with the 696cc engine. However, Rose Hill (the Austin test hill) was ascended in second gear with two up, and was still doing 20mph at the top. The following year, in the edition for 27 July 1923, *The Autocar* tested a production model with the 747cc engine. An extended road test praised the liveliness and ease of handling of the car. On many of the steepest climbs in the Midlands first gear was necessary, and in the heat wave boiling was experienced. However, no fan was fitted to the engine. Another aspect was covered in November 1925 by *The Light Car and Cyclecar*. This gave not only its assessment of the Seven on the road but also a description of how it was made. They were impressed that an engine could be assembled in a maximum of six hours or less. Engines, gearboxes and back axles were rigorously tested before assembly in the chassis frame. Further random checks were made before fitting the body, which had already had the wings and running boards fitted. The body was made from one sheet of aluminium and the floor pan from a steel sheet. Such reports must have widened understanding that mass production could mean higher standards at lower costs than traditional bespoke craftsmanship.

In 1926 *The Autocar* published an assessment of a Gordon England Sunshine Saloon. The tester questioned the long-term durability of the construction. The rather inaccessible oil filler of the magneto engine was criticised as well as the limited turning circle. The recently introduced longer gear stick was judged slightly better than the shorter, straight version. In hill tests, the car held 14mph in first up a 1 in 6 gradient and 21mph in second on a 1 in 10. First gear was judged to be sufficiently low to deal with any hill encountered.

By the time a standard Austin Seven Tourer was tested in April 1929 by *The Autocar* the tone has become a lot more benign:

> Was the word 'jolly' brought into the English language ready for the birth of the Austin Seven, or was the Austin Seven produced to give the adjective a sound reason

Prototype
Chummy, 1923.

Gordon England
Sunshine Saloon.

for its existence? There can be few motorists, old or new, in whom the handling of the little car on the road does not produce or revive pleasure.

Most babies grow up and cease to exercise their original charm, but the Austin Seven remains a little fellow, and its makers have never for one moment contemplated the great mistake of swelling into a bigger car. So it retains its charm, remains inexpensive, is still easy to accommodate, and is unswervingly economical to run. It is a car to seat two grown-up people and two children. And has never claimed to do more, but equally it can handle its official load with characteristic verve.

The tester noted that the new model (it had only done about 500 miles) ran more smoothly, especially at lower speeds, and attributed this to the greater sensitivity of coil ignition. A cruising speed of 40mph was maintained. The additional knee room provided by the flatter steering wheel and longer steering column was commended. Road holding had also improved, especially over rutted roads. Despite the clutch pedal movement being the same as on earlier cars, the tester found it 'sufficiently gentle'. Brakes were still uncoupled but the tester noted that the brake drums were now locked on the hubs with grub screws. The heavier gauge of the wheels was also approved. The tester also commented on those essentials of motoring in the 1920s: the tool kit, handbook and parts list for on-the-road attention and routine maintenance. On a 1 in 10 gradient the car climbed comfortably in second at 25–26mph, while on 1 in 6 hills first gear was required and speed dropped to 16mph. Over a hilly trial course the car averaged 38.6mph, but in easier driving conditions 45mph could be expected. The redesigned crankcase for coil ignition had the advantages that both adjusting the distributor and topping up the oil were far easier to accomplish. The scuttle now featured side ventilators and the dashboard had been given cubby holes. Wing-mounted headlights of larger diameter had been fitted, and the side screens made rattle-proof.

Ladies and a dog in a 1929 Tourer.

A new model appeared in 1929 in the form of a two-seater with a distinctive boat tail. *The Light Car and Cyclecar* report on 4 July 1930 was enthusiastic and detected a revival of interest in the 'sports or semi-sports' car and the joys of open-air motoring. Mechanically, the car was identical to the other standard Sevens. However, the 'roomy boot' housing the spare wheel was commented on favourably as ideal for stowing tennis racquets, cricket bag or golf clubs. The upbeat tone continued: 'What more could a solo motorist desire? What more, in fact, could be wanted by a man and his wife who take a delight in touring the countryside and who don't want to be bothered with the company of other people?' Alas, the time was not right for second cars merely for pleasure. The Boat Tail continued to be sold in small numbers until it was replaced in 1933 by the steel-bodied, square-backed PD Tourer.

The Light Car and Cyclecar tested an RK Saloon in January 1930. The tester appreciated the new longer gear stick and the floor-mounted hand-operated starter switch. However, he appears to have been more impressed by his visit to Longbridge Works, where he noted that more aluminium-bodied saloons were being produced than the once popular fabric bodies. Wind-down front windows were an innovation. Technically the car was the same as the Tourer but, surprisingly, the tester found the clutch 'Very sweet in action'. Despite the uncoupled brakes, the tester found that the foot brake was 'powerful, certain and proof against skidding on wet roads,' and the steering was a 'delightful feature'.

By July 1930 the aluminium-bodied saloon had been superseded by the first of the steel-bodied models. Not only had the familiar body design changed but, in the words of

1929 PA Boat Tail.

1929 RK Saloon.

The Motor in July 1930, had grown 'a half-size larger'. The new look of the steel and fabric saloons was considered to have improved the lines 'almost out of recognition'. This had been achieved by widening and shortening the scuttle, thereby allowing an increase in the bonnet length. The chrome radiator surround was taller and narrower. The petrol tank had been altered and re-sited to a ledge on the bulkhead. The tester found the body design very much better balanced than previous models, and the easy sweep from the bonnet to the windscreen pillars had taken away the 'suspicion of squareness'. The curvature of the rear panel was also noted for both looks and in providing more passenger space. The waist rail, picked out in a different colour from the body, was considered an added distinction. The body was also slightly wider and had foot wells for the greater comfort of rear seat passengers. Another improvement noted was the ease with which the windscreen could be opened and shut. Coupled brakes had been fitted, which could be adjusted by a single operation.

Another new model was tested in July 1930 by *The Motor*. This was a road-going version of the 'Ulster', and was found to have plenty of 'pep', due to its low weight of 8 ½ cwt and an engine that developed 24 bhp at 5,000 revs. The fish-tail exhaust gave 'a pleasant buzz'. The 1 in 7 of Edge Hill was taken in second gear, but Sunrising Hill's 1 in 6 ½ was found to be just too much for second. Top speed was given as 62mph.

1930 EA Sports.

The Autocar in May 1931 also tested the Ulster. The writer clearly wanted to establish a link between the other production models and the sports model:

> It is a remarkable thing that as good a miniature sport car is obtainable for the money. The owner of one of these little cars has a machine with a very fine performance, the sporting style of bodywork beloved of the enthusiast; and, most important in a way, there is behind the car a background, as it were, of extraordinary reliability and durability.
>
> Apart from the body, which complies with international racing rules as to dimensions the detail work is in keeping with the character of the car. For instance, the bonnet, which is longer than that of the normal type, has a regulation strap to secure it in place of ordinary clips; the single panel screen folds forward flat, which is a big point for the owner of a car such as this; and the instrument board carries a rev counter which, besides being exceptionally interesting in its readings, is also of real practical value.
>
> The whole feel of the car is very different from that associated with standard touring types. To begin with the frame and front axle are appreciably lower, the

springs bound with cord to stiffen them, which combined factors to give the car a genuine feeling of stability even when corners are taken fast. Further, the stiffening on the suspension, apart from its practical aspects, helps to increase the sports car effect.

On test runs 300 miles were achieved in the day and 400 miles on another day. Cruising speed was a steady 50mph at 3,500rpm. The tester could sense the power the engine was producing. The externally mounted exhaust pipe with fish tail produced a pronounced bark, which the tester judged to be 'pleasing to the enthusiast' but not enough to disturb the authorities. Oil pressure was high for an Austin Seven at between 30 and 40lb per square inch. This allowed the engine to run at over 5,000rpm, allowing up to 30mph in first and 50mph in second. It was not suited to pottering in traffic. Hills could be climbed in top gear, with a fast second gear used for the steepest hills. The closer ratio gears made it easier to change down than on standard models. Steering was light and required no effort on the part of the driver to keep on course. The advantage of coupled brakes was noted approvingly, although use of both foot and hand brake were recommended for an emergency stop. The lack of doors in the body was allowed due to the sporting nature of the car, and access described as 'quite reasonably convenient'. Despite the tester finding the steering wheel too far away, he did not feel tired or cramped after a long journey. Some criticism was made that the car had no windscreen wiper and there was no illumination for the instruments. The hood was regarded as neat, but lack of side screens was put down to the sporting nature of the car. The tail carried the spare wheel and could also be used for stowage of luggage. The test concluded:

This is one of the most fascinating little cars in existence. It has all the performance capable of satisfying the enthusiastic driver acquainted with bigger and far more expensive sports machines, yet is remarkably economical to run and easy to handle, with outstanding advantages on crowded modern roads.

In November 1931, *The Motor* tested the new long wheel-base saloon. The report found that 'the rear seat had been greatly improved: two adults of average stature can be accommodated with comfort to such a degree that even long journeys would not be arduous'. Particularly noted were the furniture hide used on the seats, with their 'pneumatic foundations', and the fitting of a sliding roof as standard. The new double-filament Lucas-Graves headlights were noted. The cruising speed was 40mph and the brakes were 'adequate when the car was driven carefully'. The excellent performance was partly attributed to the lowering of the back axle ratio from 4.9 to 1 to 5.25 to 1. The car was recommended as 'an ideal lady's car', for its fuel economy and £8 tax rating.

By 1932, when *The Motor* tested the De Luxe Saloon, heavier-gauge spokes and chrome centres had been fitted to the wheels. The petrol tank was no longer positioned under the scuttle, but mounted at the rear of the car, petrol feed being via a camshaft-operated pump. The starter motor had been repositioned inside the engine compartment, giving more floor space. The instrument panel had been redesigned, with both fuel and oil pressure gauges. A sliding roof was fitted as standard.

a7ca 1931 RN Saloon – the first long wheelbase model.

Major changes were introduced for 1933. *The Light Car and Cyclecar* approved the new four-speed gearbox, designed for starting from rest and climbing very steep hills. A new combined manifold to improve 'thermal flow' was fitted with a horizontal carburettor. The new ratios for the gearbox had been chosen 'for Average Drivers'. On test, the smoothness of the ride was such that a passenger 'calmly poured out a cup of tea from a vacuum flask and drank it without spilling a drop at 30mph'. The only criticism was of the 12-watt headlight bulbs, which were hardly adequate.

Production of the Ulster Two-seater Sports had ceased by 1932. However, the following year a new sports model appeared called the 65. *The Light Car and Cyclecar* tested the 65 in June 1933. The most obvious differences noted were the lowered suspension and the zenith down-draught carburettor. Less obvious were the chromidium cylinder head for improved combustion, the high-lift camshaft, more robust crankshaft and larger sump. In contrast to the 12bhp produced by a standard engine at 2,600rpm, the 65 engine was capable of producing 23bhp at 4,800rpm. A close ratio gearbox was fitted. Braking had also been improved and, on test, the car held the road well. The boot housed not only the spare wheel but also the pump, wheel brace, jack and jack handle, each being properly fixed in position. Other tools were carried in a box under the bonnet. The sporting appearance was

1933 RP Saloon.

enhanced by the Bluemel's steering wheel, the stone guard on the radiator and the Burgess exhaust. On test the car, which had not been run-in fully, had a best speed of 63mph. A later report in December 1933 described the 65 as 'the most inexpensive standard sports car on the market' at £148.

A successor to the boat tail models was introduced in 1933. *The Light Car and Cyclecar* report of 10 June 1933 noted that, despite it being the cheapest car in the Seven range

1933 EB 65 Sports.

at £105, the PD model was actually spacious and comfortable. Ample luggage space was available in the tail section. Full weather protection was provided, along with a hood bag. There was the usual criticism of the shortness of the clutch pedal travel; however, once underway, top gear could be engaged at 30mph and acceleration was brisk. A test on a 1 in 11 gradient showed that the car would climb comfortably in third gear, the speed never dropping below 20mph. A top of 45.5mph was achieved, with fuel consumption of 43mpg. Braking was found to be efficient, with no tendency to bind. The report concluded that it was 'quite one of the most delightful open cars at present available to those who have learned to appreciate motoring in its simplest and cheapest form'.

The evolution of the Austin continued with the introduction in July 1934 of the Ruby Saloon. This was the first of the low-frame models, due to the wheels being reduced from 19ins to 17ins diameter. *The Light Car* tested the Ruby in December 1934 and noted the sweeping changes made, while retaining the essential characteristics of the engine and chassis. The Seven had become a genuine four-seater, with comfortable headroom. Ventilation was increased by the addition of opening rear windows and visibility was enhanced by narrow pillars. The provision of pneumatic cushions and real leather for the seats was noted approvingly in such an inexpensive car. Road holding was improved by the lower chassis height. A best speed of 48.91mph was achieved. The rubber-mounted engine decreased vibration, and 45mpg was recorded. With a 20 to 1 bottom gear, the car

1934 PD Tourer.

would climb almost any hill. The gearbox had synchromesh on second, third and top gears. Braking was (enigmatically) 'about the same as that of previous models'. The instrument panel located in front of the driver was praised for its compactness. In-built self-cancelling trafficators operated from a switch on the steering column. Praise was given to the rear luggage carrier, which stowed away inside the spare wheel compartment when not in use, thus leaving the tail of the body 'entirely free from excrescences'. The report concluded that 'with its new and modernistic lines adopted for 1935, this Austin looks as good as it is'.

The Practical Motorist tested the new Ruby Saloon in March 1937 and found it 'vastly superior' to its recent forerunners. A Borg & Beck clutch had been fitted, making gear changes much smoother. The bodywork was found to be very attractive; not only could four adults be carried in comfort but up to 56lbs of luggage. The car was now promoted as 'The Silent Seven' due to the three-bearing crankshaft and rubber-mounted crankcase. In addition, the floor had been fitted with thick rubber matting and the body panels soundproofed. The four-speed gearbox with synchromesh on second, third and top was contrasted with the usual practice in low-priced cars of fitting synchromesh on only two gears. Gear changing was found to be easy, quick and sweet. The engine, thanks to the three-bearing crank, was now capable of developing 17bhp at 3,800rpm. On test, the car reached 58mph in top and nearly 40mph in third. Road holding was steady, and steering finger light. Acceleration from 0 to 30mph took 11.25 seconds and a cruising speed of 38mph in 53 seconds. The Girling brakes recorded a braking efficiency of 81 per cent on a Ferodo-Tapley meter – equivalent to a stopping distance of 37 feet from 30mph. The rear-mounted petrol tank had a capacity of 5 gallons. Fuel consumption was 43mpg, while oil consumption was considered negligible at 2,000 miles to the gallon.

Nurse with a 1937 ARR Ruby.

7

The War Years and Post-war Austerity

Despite the end of production of the Seven and the demise of the works team at the end of the 1930s, there were enthusiasts keen to continue the racing traditions. Bill Boddy, editor of *Motor Sport*, proposed in February 1939 that a 750 Club should be organised to further the achievements of the 1920s and 1930s, but as a low-cost sport for enthusiasts. An inaugural run was held on 30 April 1939 at Virginia Water, Surrey.

The start of the Second World War later the same year had one beneficial side effect. Private motoring was restricted to essential users only. This resulted in many Sevens being laid-up for the duration, thus prolonging their lives by many years. From 1945 they slowly emerged to serve as everyday transport in an age of petrol rationing and shortages. Virtually all new cars were exported. 'Make do and mend', was the motto, which encouraged ingenuity and acquisition of new skills. Staid saloons re-emerged as 'Specials', with some aspirations to sporting potential. The 750 Motor Club had been formed precisely with this type of enthusiast in mind. It would be for amateurs only and cars with engines up to 750cc. By this simple ruling the new club established the framework by which Austin Sevens did not have to compete against larger cars in the 1,100cc category. Even in wartime it had been possible to organise unofficial road, track and hill climb events, to which all types of Sevens were welcome to take part.

The 750 Motor Club and Specials

After the war there were scores of redundant airfields – ideal for circuit racing. However, it was not until the end of the 1940s and the easing of fuel restrictions that the type of motor racing events envisaged by the 750 Motor Club could get going again. Austin Sevens were plentiful, and spares cheap and easily found. Most of the work needed to build a car could be carried out using hand tools, and in an age when traditional engineering was still in demand, many aspiring racing drivers acquired their skills through apprenticeships and technical colleges.

Holland Birkett was particularly interested in using the 750 Club not only for racing but to teach young Special builders. He also suggested sharing the costs of hiring venues by grouping enthusiasts into Eight Club associations. In September 1949, 'a suggestion for inexpensive racing' appeared in *Motor Sport*. The proposals were for all cars to have side-valve engines, with the frame, rear axle, crankcase, cylinder block and gearbox built from standard Austin parts. The engine was not to exceed 750cc. Bodywork was to comply with RAC regulations for trials and rally cars. Cars were to be driven to the event. Freedom was allowed in respect of front suspension and type of fuel used. These proposals became the 750 Formula. It was the basis for many enthusiasts who later achieved fame in the world of motor racing.

One of these was Colin Chapman, whose first Lotus was an Austin Seven Special built for trialling. In 1951, he set about building a track car to comply with the 750 Formula. The Lotus Mk III used a 6ft 9in chassis but with an additional box frame over the engine. This stopped the engine from being torn apart when cornering. The engine had divided ports. With many other modifications, the car proved unbeatable, and was promptly banned by the 750MC. It took the example of Jack French to revive interest in 750 racing.

One of the most influential writers in converting Austin Sevens for low-cost motor racing was Jack French, whose articles in the *750 Bulletin* described the improvements that could be made to standard parts to improve performance. His best-known car was Simplicity Itself, which he built in five weeks at a cost of £89 in 1953. Lightweight, particularly in reciprocating and rotating masses, coupled with good brakes and weight distribution made the car outstanding in competition throughout the 1950s.

Harold Perry in the 750 Formula Special he built in 1949.

Colin Chapman, Lotus III. 1951.

Jack French and 'Simplicity', Silverstone, 1953.

Bill Williams' LMW Special, 1950s.

In his highly influential book *Austin '7' Specials* (1958), Bill Williams summarised the situation of the young post-war generation very clearly:

> Since the end of the last war, there has been an ever-increasing influx of young men – and a few women – keen to take their first steps in the world of motoring. Invariably they have started with an early Austin Seven, for in these days of high second-hand prices this popular car has been cheapest to buy and the most economical to use.
>
> This book is therefore aimed at the young members of the motoring public, who, because of their financial position, must undertake their own maintenance, overhaul and repair. It is also intended for those enthusiasts, who want something different from the next man, those who like to create by their own effort. In other words, the 'special builder'.

The MOT and the End of the Road – the Phoenix Arises

Apart from the post-war shortages of raw materials and switching from war to peacetime production, the motor industry also faced major changes in car design. The hitherto standard practice of an independent chassis carrying engine and body was replaced by the monocoque body. These new designs began to appear around 1950, but it was another decade before supply began to equal demand. Not only was car design changing, but the trunk road network had its first major upgrade since Roman times. Parts of the M1 opened in 1959. When the Seven had first appeared, dual carriageways were only just beginning to appear, and many minor roads had still to be surfaced. It was not designed for the demands of the motorway. In 1960, the introduction of the MOT placed demands on steering, braking and lighting well beyond the capacity of most Austin Sevens. The post-war market for older cars fell, and by the 1960s scrapyards were full of pre-war cars, whose former owners had opted for new Ford Anglias, Minis or Triumph Heralds.

Once again, the Austin Seven was saved from extinction by enthusiasts who wanted to conserve production cars rather than see them scrapped or chopped up to make Specials. For them, the pleasure of driving older cars was to recapture something of the fun of motoring when the roads were less crowded and the pace of life slower. While the 750 Club had been set up to cater for those interested in building and racing Specials, various other clubs appeared from the 1950s onwards catering for those more concerned with the Seven in its original forms. That did not necessarily mean absolute originality. That was not considered important by many owners.

In April 1960, a garden party was organised at Chateau Impney in Worcestershire by Bill Butler. Over 100 Austin Sevens attended, making it the first ever Austin Seven rally. This was followed in July 1963 by the first National Rally for Austin Sevens at Beaulieu, Hampshire. Most of the 186 cars that entered were standard models, and from this a separate register catering for the interests of the original Austin Seven was set up. Membership was largely drawn from South London members of the 750 Club.

Five years later, in 1968, representatives of existing Austin Seven clubs met to consider formation of an association of clubs. Those attending were the 750 Motor Club, the Vintage Austin Register, the Pre-War Austin Seven Club, the Bristol Austin Seven Club, the Austin Seven Club of Southend, the Cambridge University Austin Seven Club, the Swallow Register, the Austin Seven Van Register, the Midland Register and the Austin Seven Register. In 1969, the Austin Seven Clubs Association came into being, with the aim of promoting co-operation between Austin Seven clubs and groups, and in so doing provide a national body to represent and protect these interests. A magazine, based on the original design of the Austin Seven handbooks, would be issued quarterly to all members of constituent clubs.

However, a national association conflicted with the 750 Club, which had always been a national organisation. Some clubs who wished to join the Association were already affiliated to the 750 Club; others had no connection with the 750 Club and did not wish to affiliate. In the event the 750 Club remained primarily for racing enthusiasts and did not join the Association. The clubs mainly interested in standard cars became part of the Association and developed their own programmes of social runs and rallies.

Debate simmered for some time over how Austin Sevens should be designated. Original cars were obviously cars that had not been rebuilt, had a complete history, and all the details of chassis, engine and car number tallied with the logbook. On the other hand, Specials were clearly made up from whatever parts the builders chose to create their ideal cars. In between there lay a large group that could neither claim 100 per cent originality nor were in any way Specials. Attempts were made in the 1970s to define a replica car. However, with the passage of time, so many things have been changed on cars that nearly all are in some way non-original.

Specialist Suppliers for Special Builders

Enthusiasts now had the 750 Motor Club and the Austin Seven Clubs' Association serving their interests. However, the 1960s were the decade of the Special builders. Often after the initial expenditure on the bodyshell and a few go-fast items, enthusiasm, cash and parental approval ran out. However, there was enough interest in creating Specials for a number of small businesses to be set up to provide the parts needed to turn standard production cars into something that would go and stop a lot quicker.

By the end of the 1950s Austin Sevens could hardly be given away. Acquiring an old car had never been easier. With the *750 Bulletin* providing technical advice on how to build Specials, the beginner could gain knowledge from experts. Once a car had been found and the body removed there were firms ready to supply off-the-peg bodyshells and parts at relatively inexpensive prices.

Bill Williams had been running Auto Conversions in Willesden, London, since the 1930s, converting Austin Sevens to sports specifications. After the war he moved his business to Cambridge Road at Kew Green and became Cambridge Engineering Works. Spare parts, tuning accessories and a bodyshell based on that of the MG J2 were available.

From early beginnings in the furniture trade, Les Montgomery diversified his skills into building bodies for Austin Sevens. From this he was able to start Super Accessories in 1956. The simple ash and aluminium bodies could be purchased for as little as £22 10*s*. To assist the Special builder, lowered suspensions, radiators, Bowdenex brake kits, seats and windscreens were also offered. The booklet *The Austin 7 Special Builders' Guide* was produced.

Before founding Speedex Castings and Accessories Ltd in Luton, Jem Marsh had worked briefly for Dante Engineering. He had also already built and raced his own Speedex 750 Austin Seven. From these experiences in 1958 Marsh began offering his own versions of Dante products, such as cylinder heads, wheels and independent front suspension

Cambridge Special.

Super Accessories.

units. The same year he marketed the aluminium bodyshell he had designed for his own car, to fit both short and long chassis Austin Sevens. In 1959, a fibreglass Speedex Silverstone appeared. However, by 1962 Marsh was working with Frank Costin to produce the Ford-based Marcos and the remaining Austin-based stock was sold to Cambridge Engineering.

Ashley Laminates Ltd was founded in 1955 by Peter Pellandine and Keith Waddington at Loughton in Essex. A range of products was offered to supply Special builders, including a fibreglass Austin Seven bodyshell. Two versions were offered, designed to fit both the short and long wheelbase chassis. The short wheelbase chassis was renamed the Falcon after Pellandine left in 1956 to set up his own business.

The Hamblin Deluxe was offered from 1957 as a kit of aluminium parts designed to fit either the Austin Seven short or long wheelbase chassis, or the Ford 10 chassis. In 1968, the Hamblin Cadet fibreglass bodyshell was introduced – again, designed to fit a variety of chassis. The Cadet was made available through other bodyshell manufacturers. Modifications were required to the chassis to be used and the shell also had to be fettled first. Not all parts came with the basic bodyshell and these would have to be sourced before a complete car could be built.

Speedex.

Above: Ashley Falcon.

Right: Hamblin.

Technical Advice Sources

Throughout its production run every purchaser of a new Austin was provided with a Handbook and Parts List giving the main features of the car and technical advice on maintenance. However, for those wishing to have a little more information a number of other handbooks appeared over the years.

The Austin Seven Book by R. T. Nicholson first appeared in 1927 and was updated in 1929, 1931, 1933 and 1937. Although based on the official handbooks, the content was more diverse, covering such aspects as running costs and learning to drive. The style was less formal than that of the handbooks – more like a friendly uncle giving advice to a youngster. In 1935, the Pitman Motorist's Library produced *The Book of the Austin Seven* by Gordon G. Goodwin. The book went through four editions and numerous reprints until 1957. Later editions, written by Staton Abbey, included the Austin Eight.

Spares Suppliers

Austin continued to make and supply spares for many years after the Seven finished production. Garages usually carried a stock of frequently used items. However, the most convenient source of spares was to go to the local breaker's yard. It was part of young man's rites of passage – like train spotting and Brylcreem. It was simply a matter of turning up and searching until the part wanted was found, unbolted, and then (possibly) paid for it at the gate.

Many manufacturers offered pattern parts and other bolt-on accessories. Bodelo offered a device to convert the uncoupled brakes to operate on all four wheels. Linkula offered a gauge in place of the oil button fitted up to 1930. Oil fillers were available to create access to the rather inaccessible hole in the magneto crankcase engines. For pre-1931 cars, fuel gauges were available to obviate the need to insert a calibrated stick into the petrol tank. An alternative was in the form of petrol taps incorporating a reserve. Running board fitting petrol cans and toolboxes were also available. Other items available were knee horns, foot scrapers, radiator muffs, sun visors and mascots. Laystall offered cranks, while Remax offered cranks and half shafts. Mail order firms such as Brown Brothers carried a huge range of spares. For Londoners, retailers such as Northwoods and Elephant Motors, both in Newington Causeway, South London, offered new spares.

For those outside the London area, the mecca for new and used spares was Austin Seven Services at Kirby Wiske in Yorkshire. From 1937 until his death in 1978 it was run by John Dalby, providing a service to callers and by postal service (Mrs Dalby ran the adjacent post office). His son Chris continued the service until his own death in 2015. A visit to Kirby Wiske was an experience in itself. The sheer quantity of spares was overwhelming and the reception always friendly.

In 1968, Dave Phillips started the Seven Workshop, initially dealing in spare parts. In 1973, the business moved from its base in East London to Much Hadham in Hertfordshire. The yard was also occupied by John Heath, the specialist in reproduction Austin Seven

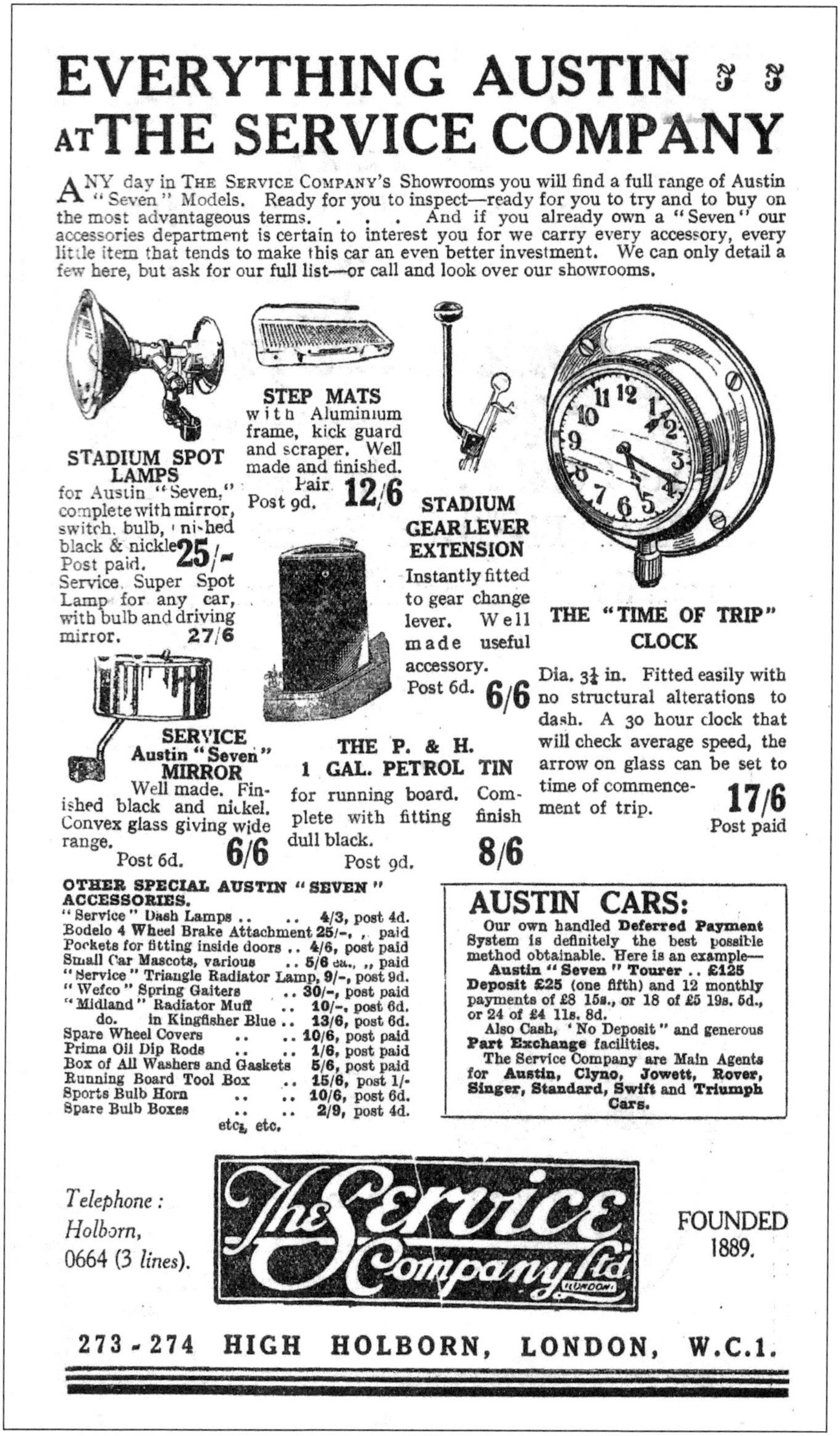

Service advertisement, 1929.

bodies. When the Seven Workshop rationalised its business to concentrate on new spares the Austineers under Dave Williams took over the used spares side, along with all repair and restoration work. The yard was sold in 1986 and both the Seven Workshop and the Austineers moved to Bradford-on-Avon in Wiltshire. The Austineers remain in Bradford-on-Avon, but the Seven Workshop has moved to North Walsham in Norfolk and is now run by Jamie Rogerson.

8

Motoring in a Seven through the Decades

There can be few places left in the world that the Austin Seven has not reached. A number of books have been written about epic journeys. Hector MacQuarrie's trip in a 1928 Chummy from Sydney to the North Cape of Queensland was achieved when no other car had made the journey successfully. John Coleman's 1959 drive from Buenos Aires to New York in a 1925 Chummy was achieved single-handed. In 1965, Clive Ball completed a round-the-world trip in a 1929 RK Saloon. In 1969, Graham Rankin and Martin Boag drove a 1932 Seven Saloon from the UK to Australia and recorded their exploits in *A Case of VAT 69* (Vintage Australian Transport, 1969). Kip and Carmen Waistell undertook the journey from Paris to Peking twice – in 2007 and 2011. Vince Leek, in his 2008 account, described six Sevens crossing the Andes from coast to coast in both directions. However, these required a good deal of planning and preparation; they were not journeys made by motorists in everyday cars for everyday purposes. Surviving accounts of everyday trips, for pleasure or necessity, offer an insight into the changing perceptions and demands made of the Austin Seven.

One such account appeared in the Austin publication *The Motor for the Million* in 1923. The writer describes a trip made in his new Chummy through the Lincolnshire Wolds. Told as a story, it persuades Jinks, a sceptical passenger, that the Chummy (at £165) is a better proposition than a motorcycle combination. After a morning on the steep and winding roads the passenger is convinced that the Chummy, far from being cheap and nasty as he supposed, was quite capable of climbing the steepest hills and putting up 45mph on the flat. By the end the passenger offers his own motorcycle combination for sale. The route is described in detail, including tramlines in Grimsby, potholes along the route, and confirms that the Austin Seven was something entirely new in performance and comfort.

In 2012, Paddy Malone recreated this run in his 1928 Chummy. His account, written in the style of the original, describes the conversion of Jinks' equally sceptical grandson of the car's capabilities. Despite improvements to road surfaces and the removal of some of the worst corners, the route remains unaltered. Ashby Hill was taken at 25mph in second gear. By the end of the ride Jinks Jr comments, 'Golly, the little car certainly attracts attention.'

2012 Jinks Run re-enactment, the hairpin at Thorganby.

A further example from the early 1920s appeared in the Austin house magazine *The Advocate*. Today motorists are less likely to encounter cobble stones, tramlines and horse-drawn traffic. Roads may have been a lot quieter, but few were surfaced. On a run from Birmingham to Liverpool the writer describes the road north of Warrington as 'one long series of potholes caused by heavy lorries, holes that would cause discomfort to the biggest car, and speed was reduced to 15mph'.

Going on holiday by car was probable unusual in the 1920s. To do so in a Chummy with parents, two children and luggage might seem a spatial challenge. However, it was accomplished for a holiday beginning in Windsor and touring the West Country:

> The suitcase itself stood on the back seat, leaving about half the seat available for the children to sit on – quite enough so long as they kept awake.
>
> The projections of the two front seats in front of and behind and the actual lockers were useful for taking safely thermos flasks, bottles of milk etc. Tennis racquets, umbrellas and sticks stood between the front seats and the sides of the car, where the inward recessing of the back wings made a good umbrella stand. The haversack went well in the centre of the back portion of the car - between the children's feet – and we spread out our coats and sat on them.

This arrangement worked excellently, as the things could be arranged and the children fitted in at the last moment.

The only trouble was when either or both of the children wished to sleep, as when they relaxed the suitcase would push them off the seat. We therefore arranged definite sleeping times for them, when their mother took one child on her lap, and the suitcase was set on end to provide proper seating accommodation for the other. This plan worked well.'

Despite the cramped conditions the journey only took eight hours, with no mechanical trouble at all. Before leaving home, a rear brake shoe spring had broken. The entire holiday was spent relying only on the front brakes.

In May 1931, *The Autocar* published the article 'Camping in a Small Car' by W. E. K. Aslin. The car used was a standard 1926 Tourer. Primus stoves and canvas buckets provided for most domestic needs. Sleeping arrangements required removal of the front seats and attachment of a piece of canvas from the back seat to the door hinge posts. A mattress was placed on top to produce, in Mr Aslin's words, 'an extremely comfortable bed'. In this way many extensive tours, apparently with happiness and enjoyment, were undertaken.

A much longer trip was undertaken by J. F. Bramley and his brother in 1928 in a Fabric Saloon. This was from Fort Augustus in the Highlands to London. By nightfall they had reached Corbridge. In the moonlight they nearly ran into a flock of Moorland sheep

1927 Chummy and family group.

resting on the roadway. They reached their home in South East London by midday, having completed 550 miles in twenty-seven hours at an average speed of 20mph.

In 1935, two brothers set off from Tenby in South Wales to drive to Dover in a *c.* 1928 Chummy. From Gloucester they took the old Roman road Northgate Street. This led to the formidable Birdlip Hill. 'We crawled carefully onwards, round the twisty bends and the elbow until the long straight to the summit opened before us. Those who knew Birdlip in those days will remember that the final agonising corner was alleged to have a 1 in 2½ gradient on the inside, which is where you had to keep on the ascent.' Having surmounted Birdlip they continued on to London where they encountered the 'new-fangled South Circular Road'. Having collected a bicycle (that being the purpose of the journey), they set off the following day along Watling Street for their home in Birmingham, covering 500 miles in three days.

Ron Peacock recalled moving house during wartime in a 1926 Chummy. Three trips were needed from Crickhowell in Breconshire (now Powys) to Godalming in Surrey. Starting at 10 p.m., Ron and his fiancée travelled the 130 miles with the scuttle headlights shrouded in the regulation hoods. On one journey he was flagged down by a motorist who asked if he had any spare petrol. This meant putting the hood down and emptying the entire car to find the can. Having received a gallon, the motorist drove off without a word or payment (1*s* 6*d* in those days). They arrived in Godalming in time to start their day's work.

By the time Maurice Wiggin recorded his experiences in *My Life on Wheels* in the 1930s the older Sevens were distinctly old-fashioned, and those who ran earlier cars were open to ridicule. Reaction to his Chummy *Whitney* in 1934 became a test of acceptability. Those who sneered at *Whitney* were rejected; those who thought the car was basically 'all right' were accepted.

At the start of the Second World War prices for early Sevens had dropped to a point where the main users were students. Ray Walker, whose garage in Perowne Street, Cambridge, was well known to generations of Cambridge University students, purchased a 1927/28 Chummy for 15*s* in 1940, with 5*s* extra for an engine with a broken crankshaft. While serving in the RAF he used it to travel to and from his posting in the north of England.

Another purchaser in 1940 was Michael Joyce, who bought a 1924 Chummy for £4 10*s* from a friend about to join the RAF. Aged seventeen and not yet a qualified driver, Michael had to put up with the jibes of his workmates. However, together with three school friends, the car was stripped and reassembled satisfactorily. War service intervened, and the car was sold for £3 10*s* to a car breaker. In 1996, the wheel came full circle and Michael again became the possessor of a Chummy.

After the war petrol rationing continued, and was not finally abolished until 1950, only to be reimposed during the 1956 Suez Crisis. In 1947, Jim Dudley in *Sevening Still* described buying a 1925 Chummy and being towed home by his father. A new BLIC magneto was supplied by the local garage for £1. Petrol had risen to 2*s* 3*d* a gallon. Unable to afford a full tank, Jim resorted to climbing one of the Herefordshire hills by lifting the back of the car to enable enough fuel to flow by gravity into the carburettor float bowl. In this way the hill was surmounted successfully.

In 1957, Peter Ward heard of 1928 5cwt van parked behind a pub for sale for £1 to anyone who would remove it. Not yet old enough for a licence, Peter and a friend went halves and

Happiness is your first car, and when it's an Austin Chummy....

Chummy no. 1, 1940, and no. 2, 1996 (Michael Joyce)

Michael Joyce in 1940 and 1996.

bought it. The friend wanted to change his mind when the engine turned out to be a pile of bits in the back. However, as apprentice fitters, his friend was persuaded that rebuilding the engine would be valuable experience. The van was pushed home and the engine rebuilt. Still without a licence, Peter tried the van out in his cul-de-sac. Stripped teeth on the crown wheel were the problem. Unable to remove the axle, the van was sold and replaced with a 1935 Ruby. Faults were identified at the MOT. The king pins were badly worn, so new ones were obtained, but the problem was the old ones had been fitted upside down. Unable to drill or punch them out, Peter bought a replacement front axle complete for £2, and brought it home tied to his back on his motorcycle. On retest, the examiner found more faults. Peter had had enough. The Ruby was sold to a breaker's yard for £2 – but only for the tyres.

The MOT introduced in 1960 and the availability of new cars combined to drive pre-war cars off the road. Mike Hodgson in *Life with Katie* described experiences common to many young men at the time. Aged sixteen, he paid £5 for a 1931 saloon, from a pile of pennies he had saved. It had been laid up at the start of the war and remained in a garden shed until 1957. Despite the years off the road, the car was started and driven home. It was not an age when respect for originality counted for much. Tyres that wore out were simply dumped with the wheel and a replacement found. Having survived the MOT in 1960, *Katie* received a set of Bowdenex cables, these being considered essential to improve braking. In the course of fitting the cables it was discovered that the u-bolts holding the front spring to the frame had come off. A further discovery was made on a journey later that the fabric coupling between the gearbox and prop shaft was only held by one nut. With these problems sorted, *Katie* managed the 147 miles from Mike's home in Worthing in Sussex to his RAF base in Church Lawton, near Rugby. The fortnightly journey was achieved in six hours. Further work on *Katie* saw a new coat of paint, then the original seats replaced by Ruby ones. The engine received a balanced crank, Cambridge head and twin carburettors. 15in wheels were fitted and better brake shoes. The journey time between Worthing and Church Lawton was reduced to three hours forty-five minutes. *Katie* had become the pride of Church Lawford, to be protected and cherished by 'the same people who would have scrapped her five years previously'.

The status of the Austin Seven in the 1960s is summed up in an advertisement that appeared in *Exchange and Mart* (eagerly awaited each Thursday in those days before eBay) for a '1932 Austin Seven Saloon, good runner, suit beatniks or clergy £10'. Clive Ball bought this car with a friend. On inspection, the car, which they named *Blodwen*, didn't look quite so good. 'The tyres were almost bald, each wheel had broken or missing spokes, and the front spring was broken. The red and black paintwork, which had sparkled on first inspection under the street lamp, was a generous crust of household paint apparently applied with a broom, and tufts of grass sprouted from the gutters and between the running boards and body.' His friend took one look, gulped, and demanded – and got – his money back. *Blodwen* survived and was fitted with a replacement back axle, Bowdenex brakes, Ruby head and manifold and an SU carburettor. These were almost standard fittings in those days.

In 1962, Ian Moorcraft purchased a nominally running 1932 saloon for £18, despite having no money, no licence and no knowledge of motor cars. His dad, unable to start the car, said, 'Chuck a match in and claim the insurance'. In total darkness, the car was backed into their matchboard garage, accidentally knocking down the prop that was holding the roof up in the process. It took four people to extricate the car the next day. Despite the poor state of the car, Ian persevered and 'improvements', 1960s-style, were carried out. The wheels were painted red, with white walls on the tyres. The seats were painted with Woolworth's green paint, the headlining was replaced with material from his mum's old skirt, and 'Go-Fast' tape was fixed to the waistline. A sign saying 'EXIT – it's way out, man' and a CND badge completed the appearance. Apart from portions of distressed bodywork, the car also lacked a starter. A stick was used in the teeth of the exposed flywheel to rotate the engine until it fired. Ian's drainpipe jeans and winkle pickers suffered in the process.

Introduced to students who were also into Austin Sevens, Ian was invited to a 'start-up' party. This was held in a first-floor flat. A newly rebuilt lime-green Chummy was in a corner

Ruby and load, 1950s.

of the room. The decision was taken to start it, unintentionally pulling up the carpet in the process. Having proved the car would go, it was dismantled, and the following evening parts were slid down a plank from the open window and reassembled at ground level.

With his own car on the road, Ian arranged to take his girlfriend for a drive. However, two of his friends and their girlfriends also turned up, and somehow all six managed to get into the car. The 1960s were the age of improvisation. A sheared half-shaft key was replaced with the two halves of a 2*s* piece. On another occasion an empty tank meant a bus trip to a garage to buy a can of petrol, but, not having a proper can, an old Golden Syrup tin was used. On the bus going back to the car, the conductor thought the bus had a petrol leak. Bald tyres were repaired with strips of canvas glued onto them. Brake linings were made from Balata belting, held on by Evo-stik and pop rivets. When the recently introduced MOT was due the tester took a benign view of the situation. Ian and *Geraldine* made it to the first Beaulieu Rally in 1963.

1932 Saloon in the 1960s.

9

The Austin Seven Motors On

By the 1970s the Seven had, with few exceptions, ceased to be used as everyday transport. Traffic was becoming heavier and speeds higher. The free and easy days of doing what you liked with an old car were over. The MOT regulations tightened and were less open to the tester's interpretation. To survive in the modern world the Austin Seven had to be roadworthy, and seek out quieter roads. Special builders had largely moved on to bigger cars, and for a time 750 racing was in the doldrums. The turning point came in 1972, the golden jubilee year, when a race for Sevens was organised at Silverstone. Although only nine cars made the starting grid, after this interest in Austin Seven racing revived, and numbers of entrants rose steadily. For standard cars originality became the criterion. Owners became interested in researching their cars and restoring them to the condition in which they left Longbridge. Specialist suppliers could provide nearly all the parts needed. The place of the breaker's yard as a source of parts was replaced by auto jumbles, often in conjunction with an event. The once plentiful supply of cars and parts began to dry up, although finds were still to be found, with luck. Prices began to rise, with the oldest cars commanding the highest prices.

The number of events continued to rise. From the inaugural run of the 750 Motor Club in April 1939 local clubs began organising social runs throughout the season. Longer distance runs became annual events. The Coast to Coast (Scarborough to Morecambe Bay), was first run in 1981. The Pennine Run (Matlock to Kelso) was first run in 1997 to mark the seventy-fifth anniversary of the Austin Seven. The Yorkshire Experience included overnight stops to give more time to enjoy the wonderful scenery. The attitude to the cars themselves had changed. Far from being regarded as museum pieces, many owners enjoyed using their cars for all manner of events, regardless of distance or hills.

The Austin Seven invites challenges. Why else would you take a car to the top of Ben Nevis or Table Mountain, across Iceland, or put a van on the top of the Senate House in Cambridge? The most popular run in the British Isles has to be John O'Groats to Land's End, or vice versa (known as JOGLE or LEJOG). The first recorded run was in 1924.

Don Rawson, Goodacre Trophy, 1962.

In 1970 Robin Newman made a successful solo End-to-End run in *Squawk*, his 1928 Chummy in thirty-three hours twenty-five minutes. To coincide with the fiftieth anniversary of the Austin Seven in 1972 Robin repeated the trip in *Squawk*, devoid of side screens, hood and the top half of the windscreen. The trip began on New Year's Day. Using the M5 and M6, and driving in appalling weather, after eighteen hours he had made it to Aviemore before being persuaded to stop, overcome with cold and exhaustion. Once recovered, he then drove back to his home on the Welsh border. He summed it up as 'a glorious failure and an unforgettable experience'. The same year at Easter over eighty Sevens attempted to complete LEJOG in under twenty-four hours – a distance of 883 miles. Leaving Land's End at midnight, Terry McGrath and Peter Thompson, driving a standard 1931 saloon, apart from a Ruby head and SU carburettor, managed to arrive at John O'Groats at 9.20 p.m. The trip had taken twenty-one hours ten minutes at an average speed of 42mph.

A challenge of a different sort was attempted in 1977 by Chris Gould and the Pre-War Austin Seven Club. A team was formed to establish the record for 10,000 miles. The idea was conceived as homage to the pre-war works team. In the best traditions, the basis for the car was a derelict Special, fitted with a much-modified Nippy engine in a box-frame chassis. The body used was one of Chris's fibreglass Ulster bodies. After much frustration a suitable circuit was found at Goodwood. Despite taking the British 5,000k record at 54.02 mph, problems occurred with the studs between block and crankcase shearing. Ingenious methods were used to try and repair the damage, including strapping the spare half-shaft across the cylinder head. The time lost on repairs meant the attempt had

Chris Gould and the Pre-war Austin Seven Club Team's 10,000 miles attempt, 1977.

Snapshots from the Bert Hadley Memorial Championship.

to be abandoned. However, the team were undaunted, and were soon planning the next attempt.

The Bert Hadley Championship has been run every year since 1992, and consists of a number of rounds, competitors being divided in to Track and Road classes.

Seventy-five years after the Speedy of John Carr and Jack Barbour had appeared at Le Mans a Speedy returned in 2010 to take part in three forty-five-minute sessions. Andy Storer and Chris Hudson finished in thirty-sixth position out of sixty-three entries, sixteenth on index of performance.

In 2012, a team entered a supercharged Ulster in the Mille Miglia. The car was prepared as closely as possible to the specification of the car that Charles Goodacre, the first Englishman to enter the race, had used in 1931. Andy Storer and Chris Hudson were again the drivers, and completed the run, including a circuit of the Ferrari test track.

National rallies have become established as part of the annual calendar, building on the success of the first Beaulieu in 1963. In August 1972, the fiftieth anniversary was celebrated at Longbridge. In 1977, the year of the queen's silver jubilee, a rally was held on the Isle of Man, with a week of driving tests. Particular efforts were made to mark the seventy-fifth anniversary of the Austin Seven in 1997 at Warwick. In 2022 the Centenary Rally of the Austin Seven is being held at Moreton-in-Marsh, Gloucestershire. Over a thousand Austins are expected to take part. The Seven is as popular now as at any time. Generations of owners have discovered the unique character of the cars. Society and attitudes may change, but a Seven goes on forever.

1931 Mille Miglia, Charles Dodson.

2012 Mille Miglia team.

Above: 1980 Archway Trial.

Below: 2009 750 MC Virgina Water Run at Brooklands.

Warwick, 2012.

Finding an Austin Seven

Of the 330,000 Austin Sevens built, over 10,000 are known to have survived. Cars are regularly advertised, prices varying on condition, model and age. Generally older and more unusual cars command higher prices. For those wishing to do a full restoration, some cars are still being found decades after they were last on the road. Such finds usually command high prices, since anything is capable of being restored. Enough chassis and engine parts are still available, and specialist bodybuilders will create any

1934 RP Saloon, with the original owner.

Sevens parade around Donington Park track, 2019.

replica car of choice. The chances of finding anything in a breaker's yard or dumped on wasteground vanished long ago, but now there are eBay, clubs and magazines to search.

Once a car has been found and brought home there is the pleasure of researching its history. With luck it will still have its original logbook and a V5C. In that case there should be no problems in getting it taxed. However, if it is not on the DVLA register, the bureaucracy of getting its original registration, or an age-related registration, approved, may require patience and perseverance. However, local club officers can provide much assistance in this matter. As an historic vehicle, the Austin Seven is tax exempt, but, confusingly, still has to be taxed annually. Insurance was at one time difficult to arrange on older vehicles, but there are now specialist insurers catering for our needs.

Mucking about in boats may be the ideal life for some, but for the Seven enthusiast nothing beats finding a car, bringing it home in triumph, and, ignoring the twitching curtains of the neighbours, discovering what treasures lie within. Years of blood, toil, tears and sweat may lie ahead. Yippee!

Making an early start on restoration.

Roger Mallinson driving his 1931 Boat Tail, which he has owned since 1958.

Appendices

Useful Contact Points

The Austin Seven Clubs Association website (www.a7ca.org) provides information on:

- Tracing a car from its chassis number or registration
- Finding a local Austin Seven club

The Austin Seven Clubs Association Archive website provides information on:

- Handbooks and parts lists
- Trophies won by Austin Sevens
- Index cards of model changes
- Personalities associated with the Austin Seven
- Paints and colours used for the cars
- Catalogue and other promotional material
- Films
- Technical drawings
- Contemporary photographs
- Identifying Austin Seven components

Other Sources of Information – Booklist

General Histories

Austin Seven by Chris Harvey (Haynes, 1985)
Austin Seven 1922–1982 (Brooklands Books, 1982)
Austin Seven Cars 1929–1935 complied by R. M. Clarke (Brooklands Books, 1982)
Austin Seven in the Thirties complied by R. M. Clarke (Brooklands Books, 1982)
Austin Seven Source Book by Bryan Purves (Haynes, 1989)
Guide to the Austin Seven produced by Practical Classics (2017)
Immortal Austin Seven by David Morgan (Veloce, 2017)

Lord Austin: The Man by Z. E. Lambert (1968)
Men and Motors of 'The Austin' by Barney Sharratt (Haynes, 2000)
Original Austin Seven by Rinsey Mills (Bay View Books Ltd, 1996)
Pre-War Austin and Austin Seven (Unique Motor Books, 2002)
Stanley Edge: His Time with Austin and Beyond by Chris Garner (2022)
The Austin Seven by D. B. Tubbs (Profile Publication No. 39, 1966)
The Austin Seven by Jonathan Wood (Shire Publications, 2002)
The Austin Seven: 1922–1939 by R. J. Wyatt (Motor Racing Publications Ltd, 1975)
The Austin Seven 1922–1939: The Motor for the Million by R. J. Wyatt (David and Charles 1972 – new edition)

Travel

A Case of VAT 69 by Graham Rankin and Martin Boag (1970)
Austins Over the Andes by Vince Leek (New European Publications, 2008)
Coleman's Drive by John Coleman (Faber and Faber, 1962)
Round the World in a Baby Austin by Hector MacQuarrie (Hodder and Stoughton, 1933)
Seven Years with Samantha by Clive Ball (Patrick Stephens, 1974)
We and the Baby by Hector MacQuarrie (Sydney A&R, 1930) – also titled *Little Wheels*

Technical

A Digest of Technical Articles from the Pre-War Austin Seven Club compiled by Mike Harris, (2002)
Austin Seven Companion by Barry Martin and members of the 750 Motor Club Ltd (1980)
Basic Fitting for Austin Seven Restorers by Chris Gould (2013)
Identifying Austin Sevens from their Factory Initials by Graham Baldock (The Austin Seven Clubs Association, 2015)
List of Production Changes complied by Dave Martin (The Austin Seven Clubs Association, 2016)
The Austin Seven Manual by Doug Woodrow (Mercury Publication Services Ltd, 1987)
The Book of the Austin Seven by Gordon G. Goodwin (Pitman's Motorists' Library, Sir Isaac Pitman and Sons Ltd, 1935) – later editions by Staton Abbey
The Book of the Austin Seven by R. T. Nicholson (Gregg Publishing Co. Ltd, 1927)
The Austin Seven Journal, Vols 1–13 (Austin Motor Co., 1927–39) – reprinted by The Seven Workshop
Tuning and Maintenance of the Austin Seven compiled by the Pre-War Austin Seven Club Ltd

Special Building

A Guide to Building Replica Austin Seven Ulsters by Chris Gould (1973)
A Guide to the Austin 65 and Nippy by Chris Gould
Austin Seven Specials by L. M. (Bill) Williams (GT Foulis and Co. Ltd, 1958)
Building a 750 Special by John Haynes (Enterprise Publications, 1955)
Building and Racing my 750 by P. J. Stephens (GT Foulis, 1953)
Tales of a Special Builder by Chris Gould

The Special Builders Guide by members of the 750 Motor Club (1959)
Would Suit Enthusiast: L M Williams and his Austin Seven Specials by Stuart Ulph (the Pre-War Austin Seven Club, 2012)

Racing

A Comprehensive History of the Austin Seven Grasshopper by Peter Hornby and Mick Hanna (Pre-War Austin Seven Club Ltd, 2014)
Austin Seven Competition Cars by M. Eyre (750 Motor Club, 1982)
Austin Seven Competition History by Beatrice Canning Brown (Twin Cam Ltd, 2006)
Austin Racing History by Roland C. Harrison (Cable Publishing Co. Ltd, 1949)
Bert Hadley, A Son of Birmingham by Geoff Roe (The Pre-War Austin Seven Club Ltd, 2013)
The Austin Seven by Bill Boddy (Grenville Publishing Co. Ltd, 1972)